FINANCES & SPIRITUALITY

Also by Doris Gothard:

THE POWER OF A NEW ATTITUDE
Email Attitude@DorisGothard.com or
To order, visit www.Dorisgothard.com
for information on other products.

SEVEN STEPS TO WEALTH
Email Wealthsda@DorisGothard.com or
To order, visit www.Dorisgothard.com
for information on other products.

ATTITUDE: THE WINNER'S EDGE
Email Attitude@DorisGothard.com or
To order, visit www.Dorisgothard.com
for information on other products.

FINANCES & SPIRITUALITY

STEPS TO FINDING PEACE, ABUNDANCE, AND FREEDOM FROM DEBT

DORIS GOTHARD

Finances & Spirituality
Copyright © 2013 by Doris Gothard

Printed by Lightning Source, an INGRAM Content Company

Library of Congress Control Number: 2013902851

Gothard, Doris.
    Finances & Spirituality.

All rights reserved. No part of this publication may be reproduced or transmitted in any form or by any means, electronic or mechanical, including photocopying, recording, or by any in-formation storage and retrieval system, without the prior written permission from the publish-er or the author. Contact the publisher for information on foreign rights.

The author assumes full responsibility for the accuracy of all facts and quotations as cited in this book.

This book was
Edited by Sue Pauling, TheTypingAnnex@aol.com
Cover Illustration by Carolyn Sheltraw
Interior Design by Carolyn Sheltraw
www.csheltraw.com
Typeset: Adobe InDesign CS5

Doris Gothard's Photo on Back Cover by
Photographer, Dr. Jeffery T. Baker, DDS SMILES by BAKER
www.smilesbybaker.com

Doris Gothard. – 1st ed.
    Biblical principles to get your finances in order /

1. Christians - Finances, personal.   2. Spirituality - Financial matters.
3. Finances - Using biblical principles

ISBN-13: 978-0-9860055-1-0
ISBN-10: 0-9860055-1-7

www.DorisGothard.com

Printed in the United States of America

To God's gift, my husband Donald…

You are so much more than just my husband…

You are my best friend, supporter, and source of encouragement.

Thank you so much for always believing in me…

and for giving me the confidence to write this book.

I love you.

Acknowledgments

FIRST, TO THE READERS OF *FINANCES & SPIRITUALITY:* This book was written to help you and your family reach your financial goals and live a good life. I firmly believe that God made it possible for me to give my first seminar on finances eleven years ago. The year was 2002. Since that time, I have been able to take this incredible journey of making a connection between our spirituality and finances (God's ownership), which leads to the truth about life. I believe God's ownership is wealth. As a result, I want to acknowledge God's ownership, which comes in many forms—a healthy body, talents and abilities, time, and yes—material possessions. The best part of writing *Finances & Spirituality* is the opportunity I have to invite all of my readers to read out loud with me the affirmation that has touched so many people who have attended one of my seminars. I believe God holds all wealth in His hands. Let's acknowledge God's ownership together right now:

- God gives us our **bodies**. We are to love the Lord our God with all our hearts, with all our souls, with all our strength, and with all our minds. (Luke 10:27, paraphrased)

- God gives us **abilities**. We are to cultivate the talents the Holy Spirit gives us in order to multiply our abilities. (Matthew 25, paraphrased)

- God gives us **time**. Whatever our jobs, we must work at them with all our hearts, and we will receive an inheritance from the Lord. (Colossians 3:23-24, paraphrased)

- God gives us **material possessions**. We are to be good stewards because God is the source of every good and perfect gift. He entrusts us with gifts and gives us the ability to produce wealth. (Deuteronomy 8:18, paraphrased)

To all of my readers, remember this: God entrusts us with gifts and gives us the ability to produce wealth; through Him we can find peace, abundance and freedom in our personal finances.

To Madlyn Hamblin, thank you for inviting me to give my first Finances & Spirituality seminar at Jackson, Michigan – the Oldest Continuous Seventh-day Adventist Church in the world. Thank you, Madlyn for inspiring me to write a book which focuses on our finances and our *spirituality*. Without Jackson, this book would not have been written.

To Sue Pauling, my editor and coach at The Typing Annex: I almost gave up writing my first book! We are now writing book number four. Thanks for your passionate, insightful comments, and feedback.

To my friend Mary Mbiya, Vice President, Flagstar Bank, Rochester, Michigan: Thank you for being in attendance during my first financial seminar 11 years ago and sharing your professional expertise in banking services. I am grateful to you for helping me to take this journey to a higher level.

To my friends and family, thanks for always being there to help me hand out materials. It is because of you that I am able to write and conduct numerous presentations.

Most importantly, I thank you, my readers, for your support over the past 11 years. Each seminar has provided me with an example of what it really means to work together with believers in ministry.

Lastly, to my husband Donald: Thank you for being my best friend, my staunch supporter, and my motivation for writing *Finances & Spirituality*. I love you because you are the last person on earth who would have thought I could write two books on finances! Thank you for pushing me to do the unthinkable – Take action to better manage my own personal finances first and write *Finances & Spirituality* to motivate my readers to take a spiritual journey to find peace, abundance, and freedom in their personal financial goals and dreams. We did it!

I am so grateful to each one of you for all of your support. Thank you from the bottom of my heart.

Doris Gothard
Washington, Michigan
March 2013

TABLE OF CONTENTS

ACKNOWLEDGMENTS. VII

FOREWORD 1

INTRODUCTION. 3

STEP ONE: CHECK YOUR EMOTIONS. 7
   Understand Your Emotional Reactions to Money . . .9
      Savers 11
      Spenders. 12
      Procrastinators 14
      Fretters 14
      Avoiders 15
      Gamblers 16
      Puritans 17
      Misers. 18
      Mixed Marriages 19
   Your Wealth Is Within You 21

    A Biblical Principle:..........................29
        The Gift of Talents......................29
        A Wealthy Thought 31
    Your Money Matters 33
        Do You Know Where You Stand? 33
    Wealth Check-Up 37

STEP TWO: BE HONEST 39
    Fears about Not Having Enough Money.........41
    A Biblical Principle: 43
        Honesty – the Best Policy 43
    Your Money Matters 47
        Do You Spend Too Much? 47
        Average Household Spending
        for a Family of Three 49
    Wealth Check-Up 52
    Household Budget Worksheet..................56

STEP THREE: GET CONTROL................59
    Define SMART Money Goals 61
    A Biblical Principle: 63
        Commitment to the Lord 63
    Your Money Matters 65
        Eliminate Credit Card Debt 65
        Know Your Credit Score 68
        Credit Score Rankings...................68
        Get Free Credit Report Updates 69
        Clean Up Your Credit Report 70
        Put More Money in Your Pocket..........71
    Wealth Check-Up 74

STEP FOUR: DO GOOD 77
Perform Random Acts of Kindness 79
A Biblical Principle: 83
    Giving Back 83
Your Money Matters 87
    Manage Your Credit. 87
    Learn How to Stand Up to Bill Collectors . . .90
    Staying Out of Debt. 92
    Good Debt. 93
Wealth Check-Up 95

STEP FIVE: PAY FOR YOUR FUTURE 97
Build a Nest Egg Through Savings
and Investments. 99
    Tips To Stop Overspending. 100
A Biblical Principle: 103
    Holy to the Lord 103
Your Money Matters 105
    Make Saving a Priority. 108
    Money Market Accounts 109
    Pretax Retirement Accounts Are a
    Great Way to Save 111
    Stocks and Mutual Funds 115
    Home/Property Ownership 119
    Steps to Creating an Investment Program . . .121
Wealth Check-Up 124

STEP SIX: BE RESPONSIBLE................127
   Take Care of Your Family and Loved Ones......129
   A Biblical Principle: 131
      Non-negotiable Standards 131
      Diligent Hands Bring Wealth 133
   Your Money Matters 135
      Be Accountable 135
      The Four P's of Responsibility 135
      Do You Have Enough For Retirement?.....138
      Living Trusts and Wills 138
      Health Insurance 142
      Life Insurance 142
      Disability and Long-Term Care Insurance...146
   Wealth Check-Up 149

STEP SEVEN: REST 151
   Accept the Gift 153
   A Biblical Principle: 157
      Be Wise with God's Gift 157
      Now is the Time to Take Action 159
   Your Money Matters 161
   Don't Panic..............................161

NEXT STEP 163

A FINAL NOTE..........................165

ENDNOTES.............................167

REFERENCES 171

Foreword

*S*TEPS IN OUR OWN SPIRITUAL JOURNEY TO find, peace, abundance, and freedom in our personal finances is an incredible journey to finding the truth about life! There are times in our spiritual lives when our vision about our financial situation becomes blurred. We see, but we do not see clearly because we are afraid. For the person who feels intimidated about finances and money - God provides a way to help meet your financial goals. The Bible says ... *"God provides us with the power to get wealth"* (Deuteronomy 8:18, NIV). I hope this book on *Finances & Spirituality* will reach and help many people meet their financial goals.

Spirituality is our own spiritual walk with God in every aspect of our lives – our gifts, our time, our talents, and our treasure. *Finances* are our management of money and our material possessions. The way we deal with our money and our material possessions says a lot about whether or not we have totally acknowledged God's power to help us meet our financial goals and provide for other necessities in life. The *gift* of God's power will help you spend less (not more!) than you make.

Bible research reveals 500 verses on prayer, fewer than 500 verses on faith, and over 2,350 verses on money. These Bible verses deal with specific ways to earn, save, spend, invest, and give money. Fifteen percent of everything Jesus said related to money and possessions. Sixteen of the 38 parables of Christ dealt with money. One of every seven verses in the first three Gospels deals with money in some way. Christ spoke about money and possessions more than about Heaven and Hell combined. The only subjects Jesus spoke of more often are love and the Kingdom of God. God uses our giving as a test of our commitment to Him.

This journey in *Finances & Spirituality* will show how Biblical principles can be used as your spiritual guide to managing your money to achieve the gift of "wealth" God has planned for you. Within this book you will read practical steps, suggestions, examples, and illustrations that you can apply in your journey. If you follow the principles as given in the Bible and referenced in this book, you will manage money without it becoming the sole focus and an idol in your life, allowing you to achieve with a clear conscience the gift of "wealth" that God will give to you. I believe this book will change lives. So, I write this with love and support to my beloved wife.

Don

INTRODUCTION

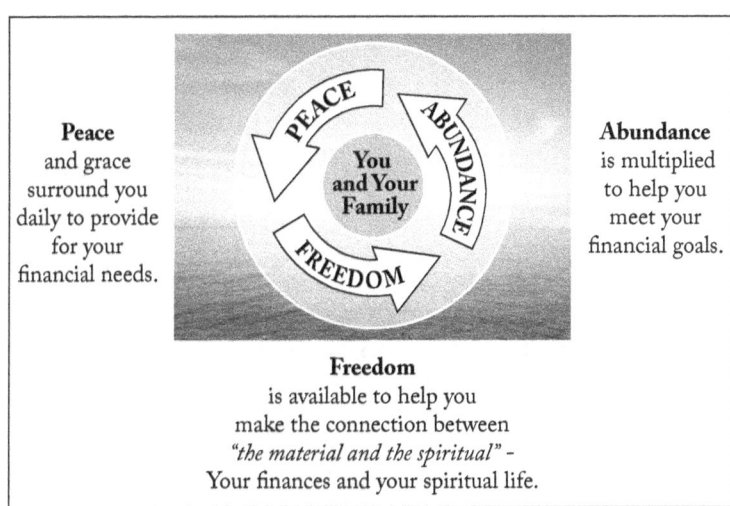

Peace and grace surround you daily to provide for your financial needs.

Abundance is multiplied to help you meet your financial goals.

Freedom is available to help you make the connection between *"the material and the spiritual"* - Your finances and your spiritual life.

Society has many definitions for spirituality whether we are religious or not. Each person knows something about a spiritual side of life.

> *"Spirituality is about paying attention to, and seeking to understand the interior life. Spirituality is about discovering the deepest longing in our lives and allowing it to direct our action. Spirituality*

resides beneath who we are and what we do, as it serves to shape who we are becoming."
– University of Portland, *http://www.up.edu/healthcenter/default.aspx?cid=989&pid=1780*

Just to be sure we all understand and agree on what *Finances & Spirituality* is about – I will offer this explanation. To have a balanced life, we cannot focus on finances (the material) and neglect the spiritual. I consider *spirituality* to be one's connection with God and a harmonious relationship with God and others. Our spirituality has a direct relationship to the truth about our finances. I have a conviction that financial wealth is more than just money alone. God owns everything. He has all power in His hands. Wealth of *any* kind comes from God. God has the power to provide us with the ability to get our finances in order.

Wealth is something most people work for because each of us has specific things that concern us, but only God has the power to give wealth. My focus in *Finances & Spirituality* will be on using Biblical principles for both spiritual and material needs. Throughout our seven-step journey in *Finances & Spirituality,* I will introduce spirituality, where appropriate, in each step. I will use Biblical principles to address not only our physical wealth but also our spiritual wealth. My goal is to integrate faith with Biblical principles that will lead us to get our finances in order and extend acts of kindness to others in need.

Why seven steps to finding peace, abundance, and freedom in your personal finances? The word "finance" has seven letters. And "7" is God's perfect number for completion. It is also enough time to get a really clear picture of how you spend money. *Finances & Spirituality* provides Biblical solutions on how to spend less than you earn and discover how your money could be doing more for you and your family.

In this seven-step *spiritual journey*, give God your best. *"Honor the Lord with your wealth, and the first fruits of all your crops; your barns will be filled to overflowing, and your vats will brim over with new wine"* (Proverbs 3:9-10 NIV). I implore you to become a "wealthy soul" by taking the journey through *Finances & Spirituality*.

This book is not intended to be a stand-alone tool. However, it is my hope that this compilation will be of tremendous help to you as you begin your seven-step journey toward financial independence. The information contained herein is not a recommendation to solve all of your money problems, but hopefully it will serve as a guide to help you understand how to manage your money better. I would like nothing more than to be with you, in person, giving a PowerPoint presentation as you take your personal journey through each step. Nonetheless, I believe a great harvest awaits you as you take your personal journey through *Finances & Spirituality!*

> *The Bible does not limit the amount of money one should aim to have, but warns against the wrong attitude toward money and possessions – such as covetousness and greed. A wrong outlook might make people obsessive, compulsive, and addicted to moneymaking (albeit honestly earned) or to the accumulation of possessions. These themes may occupy so much time and effort that they become false gods when love of money is greater than love for the Master.* [1]

Know where your heart is (see Matthew 6:21 NIV).

This book, with its Biblical principles, illustrations, and examples, will provide you with the basic awareness and knowledge to help you better manage your personal finances. May you be blessed by this spiritual journey to help you reach your financial goals. I encourage you to take the first step toward financial health, and God will provide you with the next step to financial wealth. Be blessed!

Doris

STEP ONE: CHECK YOUR EMOTIONS

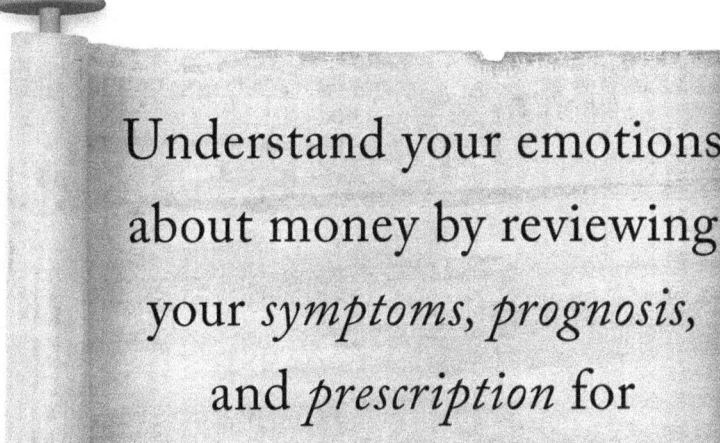

Understand your emotions about money by reviewing your *symptoms*, *prognosis*, and *prescription* for emotional spending.

Understand Your Emotional Reactions to Money

Emotions are a vital part of our personalities. They can play an important part in our overall financial well-being. As you go through the seven steps to financial freedom, meditate on each step and learn specific ways you can apply the principles contained in this book. In the end, you'll have a personal plan for keeping your emotional spending and financial goals in spiritual alignment.

No matter what our emotional ups and downs, Step One will check our emotions about money and give Biblical principles on how to better understand our emotional reactions about money and seek the power of the Lord to bring them under His sovereign control. We will look at savers, spenders, procrastinators, fretters, avoiders, gamblers, Puritans, misers, and yes, mixed marriages, focusing on our emotional reactions to money, and we will meditate and ask ourselves the important question: What can we learn from the emotional reactions of each to help us correct our own attitudes and behaviors about money? There may be some who need professional help, though in no situation should we limit the power of God to bring financial healing.

Wealth is a gift from God; what we do with that wealth is our gift to God. This seven-step journey in *Finances & Spirituality* is just a beginning. There are some intelligent findings about people that must be taken to heart. People have different emotional reactions when it comes to money. It is my hope that *Finances & Spirituality* will help us reach out to the Lord, who has bestowed on us the greatest emotion of all: love. No matter what our financial ups and downs, each of us must learn to bask in His love through this seven-step journey to financial wealth, especially during the financial downs, and then, through God's grace, share what we have learned with others.

Let's take a *medicine that cares approach* to our emotions about money and review symptoms, prognosis, and prescriptions for each emotional behavior.

SAVERS

Savers see mostly rainy days ahead. They fear that others are unreliable, and they typically don't invest their money because they're too risk-averse. They may plead poverty, but they usually have cash stashed for emergencies. Savers keep plenty of money tucked away for the long term but ignore the present.

Prognosis: Good, as long as they don't become too compulsive. Savers don't usually get into money trouble, but their reluctance to take risks can cramp their style (and that of those around them).

Did you ever wonder why people save money in piggy banks, or under a mattress, or in a jar? Does it make sense to put money in a piggy bank? Do pigs save anything? Are pigs known for being careful with their money? The truth is that a long time ago, people had inexpensive pots and jugs in their kitchens that were made of common clay, known as *pygg*. It is said that when people had some extra money, they would save the extra coin or two by putting their money into a clay container. Eventually, the containers became known as *pygg* banks, or pyggy banks. Later, someone had a great idea and began to make banks in the shape of pigs because it delighted their children.

It is a good idea to save money. However, is it a good idea to save money in a "piggy" bank? No. Keeping your money in a piggy bank, or underneath the mattress or in your pocket is not a good idea. Over time, the price of everything – from a carton of milk to a new car – goes up. It's called inflation. However, your money can't grow if you relegate it to a piggy bank. Put your money in a place where it can grow. Savings accounts and money market accounts are low risk accounts but they are paying low interest rates today. They do not give a return that will keep up with inflation but they are safe places to put your money without fear of losing it. If you have money, you should put something aside for emergencies first and then look to invest in diverse areas such as stocks, mutual funds, bonds, or annuities which have a higher rate of interest return.

Ask your bank about a money-market checking account to determine if it pays more interest than a regular checking or savings account. If so, you can use your money to make money.

Prescription: Aim for a healthy balance between planning for the future and enjoying the present. That may be hard because conventional financial wisdom says people don't save enough. However, money is also to be spent on enjoyment and fulfilling your dreams. Try to let go of the fear that you'll end up on the streets when you spend money for enjoyment.

SPENDERS

Spenders have no money focus or goals. They spend money with abandon (usually via credit cards) with no thought as to how they'll pay the debt. Sprees may occur when spenders are depressed or when things aren't going well with job or family. Spending bolsters the self-esteem, but only temporarily. Spenders often hide purchases and feel ashamed.

Prognosis: Compulsive spending can be dangerous for spenders because it's addictive and can lead to excessive debt and even bankruptcy. Most chronic over spenders had weak family relations as children and unhappy social lives in school, and often have low self-esteem. Some women tend to attach themselves to men who need to be taken care of. Women often will buy men gifts, pay their bills, etc. Some men typically get into debt buying things for themselves. A lot of spenders pay for cars that they no longer possess. Spenders are more often than not trying to impress other people.

Prescription: Pay yourself first! Put your money in a savings account where you can't see it. Spenders should start by having a reasonable amount withheld from their paychecks for emergencies in a bank savings or money market account. Spenders should save by making direct-deposits into an account for retirement savings. Spenders should also work on their spending habits. Confess to yourself, your partner, or a close friend that your spending habits are out of control and ask for financial assistance. Cut up all but one major credit card. Stay out of stores where there's a chance you'll buy items you don't need. If you're overcome with the urge to shop, take cash – the amount you can afford to spend – and make it a very small spree. Write down every item you feel is necessary to purchase; it will help you gain insight into your spending behavior.

PROCRASTINATORS

Procrastinators fail to pay taxes or bills on time. They do not prepare budgets, keep any records, or record spending habits. Procrastinators may not save funds for retirement. They may not have life and/or disability insurance. They believe financial planning will take care of itself.

Prognosis: The outlook for the procrastinator isn't as bad as one might think. Financial planners say there's some form of procrastination in all of us. All we have to do is get off the dime and take the first step.

Prescription: Procrastinators should take one step at a time. Plan to spend time each day pulling together financial records and then once a week thereafter keeping them in order. If you're a procrastinator, make an appointment with a financial planner who can help you get going.

FRETTERS

Fretters obsess about money. Fretters feel immobilized by fear of poverty. They fail to enjoy anything money buys – dinners out, gifts, entertainment, shopping trips, and vacations.

Prognosis: Fretters don't get into big financial trouble, but their money quirk prevents them from enjoying life fully and can cause trouble in their relationships with others; of all the money problems, fretting and compulsive saving may be the least disruptive money approaches and probably have the best chances of being cured.

Prescription: When you go out to a restaurant for dinner, do you keep talking about the cost of the meal prices? That's no fun for you or your dinner partners. The next time you go out to a restaurant for dinner, focus on the food, the conversation, and the atmosphere. Don't mention or even think about the cost.

AVOIDERS

Most avoiders shun all forms of risk. They refuse to change jobs or move. Avoiders may turn down job opportunities because they fear failure. Avoiders never invest in the stock market because they fear the risk of losing money.

Prognosis: Of all the money behaviors, risk avoidance is the one most likely to be inborn. Some people are just more risk averse. Others are terrified of financial loss because they've already suffered a serious emotional loss. Avoiders just can't bear to take the risk. The good news is risk avoidance behavior that has been learned can be unlearned. Expect change to be slow and be prepared to work on it.

Prescription: Draw up a list of things you consider to be risky, starting with the most risky. They can be career-related risks, relationship risks, or investment risks. Pick the item at the bottom of your risk list and come up with ways to eliminate as much risk from it as possible. If a shopping trip to the mall is the last item at the bottom of your risk list, you can eliminate risk by taking cash versus a credit card. You will spend the amount you can afford and make it an enjoyable "low risk" shopping experience.

GAMBLERS

Gamblers need excitement. They believe that lucky socks, the right hat, or turning around twice before getting into an elevator will bring the Fates into line. Gamblers get a thrill out of taking chances at the racetrack, the blackjack table, or the stock market. Winning boosts their self-esteem; they may feel compelled to gamble when losing.

Prognosis: Addicted gamblers need to join Gamblers Anonymous or get professional help, but investors who typically make risky investments and then lose big can profit from a little introspection. For example, it has been shown that many doctors gamble because they feel deprived because of their long and arduous training period.

Studies have proven that many doctors have this sense of pressure to catch up. They are trained to make snap decisions in life-and-death situations and tend to do the same with their material possessions (investments).

Prescription: Gamblers should step back and think. Step back from your material possessions (investments). Don't use them as a mirror for your self-esteem. One of the biggest dangers for gamblers is pulling out of an investment as soon as it starts losing. It is important to remember that stocks go up and down. They don't stay the same. The goal should be to pick one or two solid investments, research them well, and stay the course for the long period. There's no reason to make seat-of-the pants decisions because plenty of information is available about stocks and bonds on the Internet or in magazines such as *Money Magazine*, etc.

PURITANS

Puritans believe that money is for necessities only. They see frugality as a virtue and spending for fun as sinful. Puritans may be threatened by success and overcome by guilt if they earn too much. They are embarrassed if given an expensive gift. Inheriting money can be a big problem. Typically they're not prone to invest. They have a terrible time investing.

Prognosis: Not bad. The Puritan's approach would be okay were it not for the fact that we all need money to achieve some of our goals and dreams. The conflict for the Puritan is if having money is bad, then saving (hoarding) and investing it are even worse.

Prescription: Making money is one goal in life but should not be the highest goal. There are people who are financially wealthy but still admirable. For example, Sir John Templeton, multimillionaire founder of the Templeton family of mutual funds, established the "Templeton Foundation Prize for Progress in Religion." Sir John Templeton was blessed with the gift of financial wealth and he used his gift of wealth to glorify God and extend acts of kindness to others in need – an example of "doing well" and "doing good."

MISERS

Misers tuck away every penny that comes in, invest very carefully, and mistrust others. Possessing money provides feelings of safety and security; spending gives a sense of inner depletion and loss of power. At the extreme, misers amass more money than they will ever use.

Prognosis: True misers almost never go into therapy. They don't realize they have a problem (and besides they don't have to pay for it). Misers will bring home leftover rolls and packages of artificial sweetener from restaurants and yet are worth millions.

Prescription: Make a list of things you might enjoy but feel are too extravagant. Then buy one thing – a new book or flowers. Wait a week. Then buy something a bit more extravagant – a dinner out, a silk tie or scarf. The sky won't fall, and you may even enjoy yourself.

MIXED MARRIAGES

Most marriages are mixed when it comes to approaches about money. Most couples rarely have the same goals or approach decision-making in the same way. What happens when a person ends up with a partner who has the opposite approach? Although a gambler and an avoider might have squabbles, a compromise can make for a healthy money relationship. There are times when both partners may have jobs in the financial business, but they take different approaches to their own money. Perhaps she's extremely conservative and eager to be completely debt-free while he makes a great case for stretching out mortgage payments to take advantage of a larger deduction.

Prognosis: It is critical in the decision-making process that each partner respects the other's style and is willing to compromise. A solution in a mixed marriage might be to make an additional lump sum payment on the mortgage each year to reduce the mortgage principal. Compromising also means the ability to recognize that money decisions are more than just dollars and cents. There are two personality types to consider when it comes to money decisions. One is the "thinker" who adds up all the numbers and does things very methodically. The other is the "feeler" who never balances a check book, never writes or adds anything up but says, "It feels right so I'm going to do it."

Prescription: The two personalities need not be incompatible providing they understand each other's approach. This sort of understanding comes from honesty – the key to a good financial relationship in mixed marriages. When couples reach an impasse over a financial decision, it usually indicates that something deeper is going on. It is a signal that you need to sit down and talk about your goals and priorities and how each of you defines success.

RECAP

So far, we have learned some things about ourselves and other people. Let us take these lessons to heart. We all have different emotional behaviors when it comes to money. But, there is a little bit of saver, spender, procrastinator, fretter, avoider, gambler, Puritan, and miser in each one of us. Let's take a *medicine that cares* approach to our emotional attitudes about money to better manage our finances. Let's learn the symptoms and gain a better understanding of the prognosis. God will write the prescription to change your bad money habits into good money habits.

Your Wealth Is Within You

Understanding your attitude about money is one part of looking inside yourself. Another part is understanding how you came to hold that attitude. I encourage you to think back to your childhood. Think back! The memories you have about money from your childhood to adulthood will teach something about who you were then and who you are today. Subtle messages are passed down from one generation to the next in much the same way clothes are passed from older siblings to younger siblings.

Most of our thoughts actually create fear that paralyzes us when we think about not having enough money to pay the bills. Often we regret that we did not treat the money we had like a cherished friend. When we treat people with value and respect, they will work for us and will buy whatever products or services we sell. Likewise, when we give our money the respect it deserves, our money will work for us, and we will always have enough to meet our needs.

At times, parents may appear to be unhappy, but most often it is not because they don't love each other—it is because there is not enough money to pay the bills. If we desire to become debt-free, we must learn to protect our money and not allow destructive emotions to blow it away. When we think about our responses to money, we respond in one of several ways: we enjoy it, we love it, or we hate thinking about it. Remember to look inside – the key to a future of wealth is inside of you.

Think back! Think back to your childhood and look inside! Think back to when you were five, twelve, or sixteen. Identify one memory about money (good or bad) that was important to you. Thinking back will help you begin to remove your personal fears about money; it will help you break free from your personal roadblocks about your finances and will help you address your fears regarding money. Take a few moments to ask yourself the following questions:

- Did your parents tell you things about money that made you feel good?

- Did your parents talk to you about the importance of saving money?

- Did you receive presents as a child?

- Did your school friends have things you didn't?

- Did your mother have to work?

- Did you get money every time you went to see your grandparents?

- Were you ashamed to bring your friends home to your house?

- Did you have to be good in order to earn rewards?

- Did you feel like your friends had nicer clothes than you did?

- Did your parents have a car?

- Did your friend's parents have cars?

- Did you feel ashamed of having far less than your friends?

The following testimonials were written by students who have already taken a seven-step spiritual financial seminar. They voluntarily wrote about their childhood memories about money in the hope that one day, this book would be published. I hope their memories will help you talk about your fears about money and remove any roadblocks to your financial freedom.

> *My father always kept money in his wallet. His theory was that if you were as ragged as a church mouse but had $500 or $600 in your pocket and some in the bank, then you were Mr. Somebody. My father worked hard, knew how to do many different things, and always had money. When people were in need, they borrowed money from him. I thought that act was crazy. So – I knew that I didn't want to do the loaning because people got paid on Friday and had to borrow on Sunday a.m. – Senseless!! The lesson that stuck with me was to save something out of every check for a rainy day.*

> *At seventeen, I was married and had my first child on the way; I had to finish school because mother would have it no other way. I fell into the same trap most young ladies in the South sometimes do, thinking Mr. Wonderful would save you. But, in reality, you wake up and find out you are responsible for yourself. There is no man who can save you—only God can save you. I learned you cannot have a home – eat – have clothes – go places and do things – on LOVE. You must have money. My first memory of money was this: You need money to survive. So, I have always worked. I keep a job. And by the grace of God, I move forward, trying hard not to go back-*

ward. I make mistakes, but I get up and keep going.

At age 7 I saw a dress I wanted and asked my father to buy it. He said he didn't have the money. That was fine until my sister asked for money for boots on the same day and she got them. I was very upset and said I would make my own money and buy what I wanted. I began collecting store sales receipts to turn in for money, doing chores for neighbors, collecting bottles for refunds, etc. Eventually, I got a paper route. I continued to work from a very young age and never asked my father for anything until high school, and that was to go to college because he had said that he would send the first kid to graduate to college. I was the youngest but the only one to graduate. However, he told me he didn't have the money for college. That crushed me. At 17, after graduation I moved away from home to never return, no matter what I endured. My father continued to do for my sister until his death. She never worked until she was 35. I saved a little money and bought my cemetery plot at 24. People thought I was crazy. At 24, I had invested in mutual funds and was preparing diligently until I hit my 40s. I then became reckless with my finances and I am paying for it to this day. Slave to debt!

It was a Saturday in the summer of 1949; most of my friends were all excited about going to the mov-

ies that afternoon. They were going to see the movie <u>The Gunfighter</u> starring Gregory Peck. I don't remember caring about the movies until that time. It cost $.12 to get in the theatre and though I hustled by depositing bottles and flat out begging, my best effort yielded only $.11. I watched as my playmates cheerfully marched and faded into the distance towards the theatre. I sat on my porch with my head in my hands ... propped on my knees ... and cried.

I remember living in a big house, but we still did not have money to pay our bills. I remember my mom crying one night because my dad had gambled away the savings.

My mother and father were arguing about money. Daddy had walked out the door, and mother was about to lock it. He busted back into the door, hitting my mother with it and knocking her into the opposite wall. She was lying on the floor with her head bleeding. This is my early memory about money.

Once while living with my grandmother, I asked for a bike for Christmas. I was tired of walking to school and wanted to be like the other kids. Well, Christmas came and I looked all over for my bike. But there was no bike. I asked my Grandmother why didn't I get the only thing I had asked for. She looked at me calmly and said, "You never once asked *me if I could afford a bike." That introduced me to a reality that everything we wish for, want for, pray for, or plan for does not always come unless we truly can afford it. I have since returned things I could not afford and did not plan for only to get deeper into debt trying to hold on to things. I only wish I sought the wisdom my grandmother had.*

A BIBLICAL PRINCIPLE:
INSPIRATION TO HELP YOU MEET YOUR FINANCIAL GOALS

Within you is at least one God-given gift or talent of money, perhaps more. God wants you to "look inside" to find your talent and use your talent as a channel of His blessings. Let's take a look at a parable about God's gift of the talent of money to be used.

THE GIFT OF TALENTS

Matthew 25: 15-27 (NIV) says,

> *To one he gave five talents of money, to another two talents, and to another one talent, each according to his ability. Then he went on his journey. The man who had received the five talents went at once and*

put his money to work and gained five more. So also, the one with the two talents gained two more. But the man who had received the one talent went off, dug a hole in the ground and hid his master's money.

After a long time the master of those servants returned and settled with them. The man who had received the five talents brought the other five. "Master," he said, "you entrusted me with five talents. See, I have gained five more." His master replied, "Well done, good and faithful servant! You have been faithful with a few things; I will put you in charge of many things. Come and share your master's happiness!" The man with the two talents also came. "Master," he said, "you entrusted me with two talents; see, I have gained two more." His master replied, "Well done, good and faithful servant! You have been faithful with a few things; I will put you in charge of many things. Come and share your master's happiness!"

Then the man who had received the one talent came. "Master," he said, "I knew that you are a hard man, harvesting where you have not sown and gathering where you have not scattered seed. So I was afraid and went out and hid your talent in the ground. See, here is what belongs to you." His master replied, "You wicked, lazy servant. So you knew that I harvest where I have not sown and gather where I have not scattered seed? Well then, you should have put my money on deposit with the bankers, so that when I returned I would have received it back with interest."

The message is this: Money is a talent to be used. God wants to multiply your talent of money. You have an opportunity to use the talent of money you have been entrusted with to *gain* more talents of money to use in His service!

A WEALTHY THOUGHT

Money is a talent to be used. The one who received five talents of money ($1,920,000[1]*) used them to get five more talents which earned an additional $1,920,000*. Likewise, he who was given two talents of money ($768,000*) used them to get two more talents which earned an additional $768,000*. But, the one who received **one** talent of money ($384,000*) did not use his one talent to get one more talent. He said he was afraid and he went and hid his talent in the earth. The one who hid his talent increased his value by $0 because he did not use the **one** talent he was given to earn more talents; he was afraid and content to hide his talent. God told him to be fruitful and multiply his talent – not hide his talent in the earth!

The message is this: Look inside. God wants to multiply your talent of money. Do not be afraid to use the talents

---

1 *Note: An easy-to-understand alternate meaning of talents.

you are given to learn ways to handle your money better. Money is a talent to be used for His service.

Your Money Matters
Discover How Your Money Could Be Doing More

DO YOU KNOW WHERE YOU STAND?

Your money matters. It's important for you to understand its value and your current situation in order to determine how and where you can make improvements. First, let's make the connection about money. How do we use our money? What motivates us to spend? Take a moment to examine some of the following motives:

- We buy to <u>heal</u> wounds.
- We buy to <u>satisfy</u> others.
- We buy to <u>prove</u> something
- We buy to <u>keep up</u> with the Jones'
- We buy to <u>be happy</u>.
- We buy to <u>look good</u>.

- We buy to <u>impress</u> people.
- We buy because of a <u>need</u>.

The first step to knowing where you stand is to talk to your family members about finances. Set up weekly chats. These chats don't need to be long. Talk about the basics—your monthly budget, income, bills, checking account, savings, and so on. Approach your family chats in a positive way, otherwise you may overreact to family members about money. Make sure you have a plan. Set up a monthly budget. Keep track of your spending so money doesn't disappear from your pocket. Remember to organize your money: $1 bills together, $5 bills, $10 bills, etc. This way, you will know if any of your money ever goes missing. These topics will be addressed in depth in Step Two.

The path to financial success is much like being mired in a deep malaise. *Malaise* simply means an uneasiness or discomfort. For example, this can apply to feelings of uneasiness and discomfort about finding a job after graduation from college. Every parent dreams that their children will grow up to be hardworking citizens and make a positive difference in the world. After years of wandering in the wilderness, my only son finally woke up and said, "Mom, I am sick and tired of being sick and tired. I am going to go back to college and get my degree." This was a life-changing experience for me to hear these words. Four years later, he graduated from the university with a B+ average. The joy of his graduation soon turned into uneasiness and discomfort because his graduation came at a time of financial crisis across the country. To this day, he is still unemployed and looking for a career position. This has been an emotional malaise for many college graduates who are still looking for that career job opportunity! There are many reasons for emotional and financial malaise: a down economy, loss of jobs, smaller raises, high unemployment, businesses being afraid to hire, fruitless job hunts, retirements being delayed because people are working longer.

During the battered down economy in 2010, retail vacancies cropped up throughout the country and became a revolving retail door. Empty storefronts along streets and many ritzy stores felt the pinch of the economy. Houses languished on the market, and a glut of homes took their toll on anxious would-be-sellers. Higher gas prices hurt the demand for SUVs. There was targeted downsizing and restructuring of auto plant facilities in North America and Europe to build smaller vehicles.

In a down economy there are smaller raises and high unemployment. Most businesses are afraid to hire in a down economy. Auto companies and suppliers are looking at possible bankruptcy. Thousands across the country are without jobs. However, be comforted! In *Finances & Spirituality*, there are solutions to a financial malaise. Some of the things you can do include becoming conservative in your spending habits. Brave souls spend less. Penny pinching can pay off. Change the way you handle your money.

Put off major purchases. When you change your attitude about money, you may want to trade your SUV for a smaller, more fuel-efficient and economical (smaller?) vehicle. In general, spend less. You'll have more. Our attitudes about money and our childhood memories about money affect how we handle money today. These topics will be addressed in depth in Step Two.

WEALTH CHECK-UP

Which of the following best describes your financial goals?

❑ I do not have any real financial goals.

❑ I have some financial goals but I do not know how to make them come true.

❑ I have some financial goals and I have created a plan to make them come true.

❑ I have some financial goals and they are coming true.

Write Your Financial Goals

My Goal is _____

_____

_____

_____

_____

Examples: My goal is to pay off my _____
and _____.

I want to have enough money to retire in _____ years.

Do you have any dreams that you want to see come true?

My Dream is _____

_____

_____

_____

_____

STEP TWO: BE HONEST

Be honest with yourself. Don't bend the truth about YOUR finances.

Fears About Not Having Enough Money

OUR FEARS ABOUT NOT HAVING ENOUGH money affect our ability to manage our finances. Most people have anxieties about money and carry these anxieties around with them, though they may not admit it to themselves or others. Here in Step Two, I encourage you to be honest about your finances. Financial freedom is achieved when we take steps to overcome financial difficulties. We move beyond the pain and the fear of not having enough money and not taking any action. When we ask in *faith*, we can overcome any financial difficulty through faith.

The mind gives us thousands of ways to say no. The heart gives us only one way to say yes. Most people feel paralyzed when it comes to actually treating the money that they have with respect like a cherished friend. It is best to look the money that you have in the eye, face your fears, and reclaim your power. Retrain your mind from thinking you can't control your finances. Retrain your mind from thinking you don't deserve to be successful. Retrain your mind from thinking that not enough money is going to come when you need it. Retrain your mind to think, "All things are possible, and I will be able to support my family and have financial freedom." In order to retrain yourself, however, you must first be honest about your finances. This is the next step in acknowledging God's ownership and embracing the knowledge that wealth is a gift from God, and what we do with that wealth is our gift to God.

A Biblical Principle:
Inspiration to Help You Meet Your Financial Goals

HONESTY – THE BEST POLICY

"For we are taking pains to do what is right, not only in the eyes of the Lord, but also in the eyes of men" (2 Corinthians 8:21 NIV).

> *My son Will once found a $100 bill at a store before Christmas. Recognizing this as a perfect teaching moment, I guided him to the customer-service desk. They assured him they would contact him if no one claimed the cash. He just knew luck would not be on his side. One day a woman called to thank him. She said it was all she had for groceries and her kids' Christmas gifts. Still, she wanted to share $10 with my son.*

Later one of Will's schoolmates asked if he was the guy who'd turned in the $100. When my son replied yes, the boy looked up shyly and said, "That was my family who lost it. Thank you." At the dinner table that night, tears were in Will's eyes as he told his story. (Kay-Cee Cruzen as told in Reader's Digest, June 2001, pp. 17-18)

The honesty and compassion displayed by this young man reminds us of the trust that God has placed in us by placing material gains into our hands, and that He asks only that we trust Him and return an honest tithe to Him. *"'Test me in this,' says the Lord Almighty, 'and see if I will not throw open the floodgates of heaven and pour out so much blessing that you will not have room enough for it.'"* (Malachi 3:10 NIV) [2]

Be honest with yourself. Don't bend the truth about your finances. Know how much money you are spending each day. Know how much you are spending each week and each month. If you can admit that you are wasting $5.00 a day, commit to saving it! Turn your waste into wealth ... by saving $5.00 a day.

Proverbs 24:26 (NIV) says, *"An honest answer is like a kiss on the lips."* One who gives an honest answer is wise. One who bends the truth is foolish. Honesty is the best policy. *"For we are taking pains to do what is right, not only in the eyes of the Lord, but also in the eyes of men"* (2 Corinthians 8:21 NIV).

The message is this: Honesty is the best policy. Be honest about how you manage your money. Spend a week tracking all of your expenses, and then create a budget that allows you to both meet your needs and begin some savings. No matter what the cost, you will receive the *gift* of financial freedom when you live on a budget and stay on a budget!

Your Money Matters
Discover How Your Money Could Be Doing More

DO YOU SPEND TOO MUCH?

Most people underestimate what it really costs them to live each month. The key to knowing how to estimate actual living expenses is to keep track of cancelled checks, bank cash withdrawals, and money spent every month as well as money spent once a year (money spent for birthdays, baby showers, and holidays). Your bank account and your bills contain the key to how you live your life. The total amount of money you are reasonably sure will continue to come in each week or each month is called your income. The total amount of money you spend, recorded on cancelled checks, bank cash withdrawals, plus the money spent every month and every year for showers, weddings, holidays, vacations, and monthly bills tells you how much you have going out.

Most people spend more than they think they spend. In order to have financial freedom, you must decide to spend less or make more money.

Do you love your credit cards? *"The rich rule over the poor, and the borrower is servant to the lender"* (Proverbs 22:7 NIV). Do you want to live a prosperous life? The borrower must realize that until the credit card debt is repaid, he is a servant to the individual or institution that made the loan. Credit card debt we can handle is enabling; debt we can't handle is enslaving. Never put charges on a credit card without carefully examining your ability to repay it.

"Dear friend, I pray that you may enjoy good health and that all may go well with you, even as your soul is getting along well" (3 John 1:2 NIV). You know that you are not living a prosperous life but are living above your means when…

- Your unpaid monthly credit card debt is greater than your tithe per month.

- Your auto loan payment is greater than your tithe per month.

- Your mortgage/rent is greater than 25% of your gross income per month.

For example, assume you have a monthly income of $2,000. Twenty-five percent of that amount is $500. If your mortgage or rent is more than $500/month, then you are living above your means.

The key to financial freedom is to have a budget. *"The plans of the diligent lead to profit as surely as haste leads to poverty"* (Proverbs 21:5 NIV). With a budget, you set a limit for what you can spend each week or each month. Make a decision to choose how you want to spend the money you have each month. It is important to know how much is coming in and how much is going out! A budget will be your roadmap to reaching the goals you have for your money.

AVERAGE HOUSEHOLD SPENDING FOR A FAMILY OF THREE

The following chart summarizes the average household budget in 2009 for a family of three in the United States according to the U.S. Department of Labor:[3]

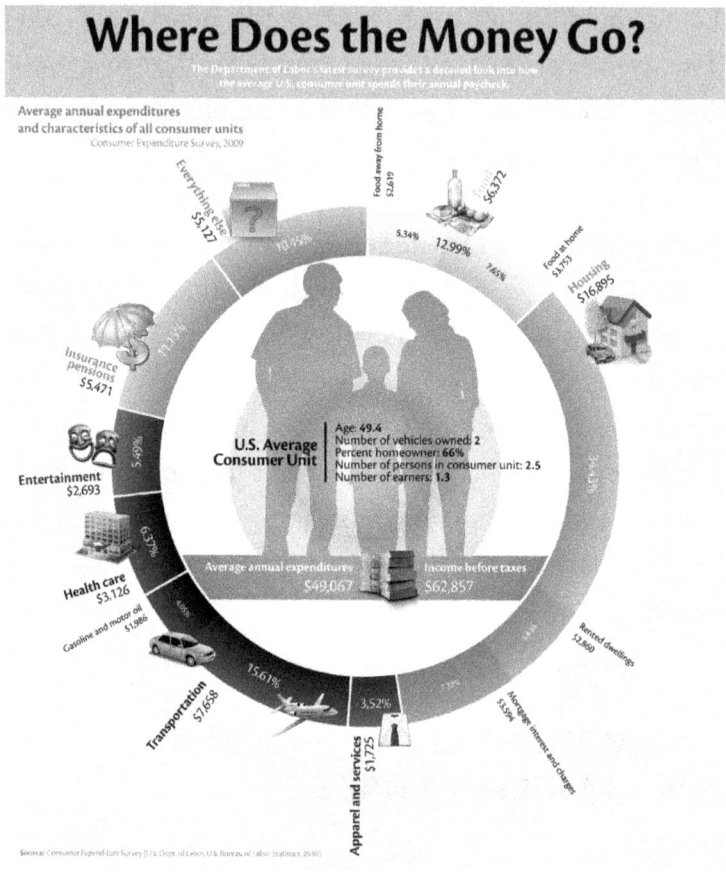

This chart describes a typical annual household budget for the average American family. The largest annual expenditure is housing at 34.1%. The second largest expenditure is transportation (17.6%). Other large expenditures are money spent on food, insurance/pensions, healthcare, entertainment, and clothing. The chart represents how we tend to spend our money.

Here are some tips for setting up a household budget (it's all in the family!). Budgeting works better when each family member gets involved. If family members are included in the budgeting process, they will be more inclined to make an effort to make sure the budget is followed. Sit down with the rest of the family and assess everyone's financial needs and contributions. Decide together your priorities. Each family member should keep a close record of all the expenses, no matter how small, to get an idea of where money is going on a daily basis. Also, life is filled with the unexpected. I encourage every family to allocate $50 to $100 each month for miscellaneous unpredictable expenses. Review your budget regularly to measure progress and identify changes that may need to be made.

To recap, you need to be honest. *"For we are taking pains to do what is right, not only in the eyes of the Lord, but also in the eyes of men"* (2 Corinthians 8:21 NIV). Build a budget. Keep track of the money you get each week, and then keep track of the money you spend. If there is no extra money each week, start a plan to spend less each week and save the extra money for things you really want. Know where you stand financially. There is a budget work-sheet provided for you at the end of this chapter.

WEALTH CHECK-UP

Which of the following best describes your attitude about a monthly spending plan or budget?

❑ I do not have enough money to have a budget.

❑ I would like to have a monthly budget, but do not know how to make one.

❑ I have a budget for the monthly bills but not for everyday expenses.

❑ I have a monthly budget and I use it to plan for all of my monthly expenses.

Which of the following best describes your attitude about your bill paying practices right now?

❑ I pay my bills on time.

❑ I occasionally pay my bills on time.

❑ I hardly ever pay my bills on time.

❑ I do not pay the bills in my household.

FINANCES & SPIRITUALITY

Answer "Yes" or "No" for each of the following. Does your response to each question maximize your saving potential?

1. Do you have a long-term savings plan?
   _____

2. Do you have an emergency fund?
   _____

3. Do you buy a custom car license for your car?
   _____

4. Do you order and use custom checks from banks?
   _____

5. Do you have a NO interest checking account?
   _____

6. Do you pay for premium channels on cable TV?
   _____

7. Do you avoid using discount coupons?
   _____

8. Do you leave lights on in rooms you're not using?

   _____

9. Do you turn your heat down at night?

   _____

10. Do you pay interest charges on your credit cards?

    _____

11. Do you use premium gas in your car vs. regular gas?

    _____

12. Do you buy at the supermarket without calculating the lowest cost per unit size in whatever brand you are buying?

    _____

13. Do you have telephone services that you don't use?

    _____

14. Do you buy your lunch at work?

    _____

15. Do you shop for food when you are hungry?

    _____

16. When buying merchandise that's not on sale, do you ask if it will be going on sale soon?

    _____

17. Do you refuse to buy store brand products?

    _____

18. Do you buy only designer labeled clothes?

    _____

19. Are you renting your place of residence?

    _____

20. Do you eat out more than twice a week?

    _____

21. Do you have a basic manual thermostat for heat control?

    _____

22. Do you keep your emergency money in a bank savings account?

    _____

Doris Gothard

Household Budget Worksheet

	Current Spending	Yearly Total	Monthly Budget
INCOME	$	$	$
Take-Home Pay			
Social Security			
Investments			
Total Cash Available	$	$	$
EXPENDITURES	$	$	$
Mortgage/Rent			
School Loan			
Car/Truck Loan/Lease			
Other Loan(s)			
Investments/Savings			
Transportation:			
Gas			
Maintenance			
Car Insurance			
House Insurance			
Gifts			

Finances & Spirituality

School			
Hobbies			
Vacations			
Credit Card(s)			
Donations:			
Church			
Fundraisers			
Community projects			
Other			
Entertainment:			
Movies/concerts			
Restaurants/night clubs			
Sporting events			
Cable			
Clothes and Footwear:			
Clothing			
Shoes			
Laundry/dry cleaning			
Miscellaneous:			
Cleaning supplies			
Housewares			
Home maintenance			
Soaps/detergent			
Medical:			
Insurance			
Services			
Medicine			

Utilities			
Electricity			
Gas			
Telephone(s)			
Water/sewer			
Taxes:			
Federal			
State			
City			
Health Club			
Beauty Care			
Total Expenses	$	$	$

Shortfall/Surplus	$	$	$

STEP THREE: GET CONTROL

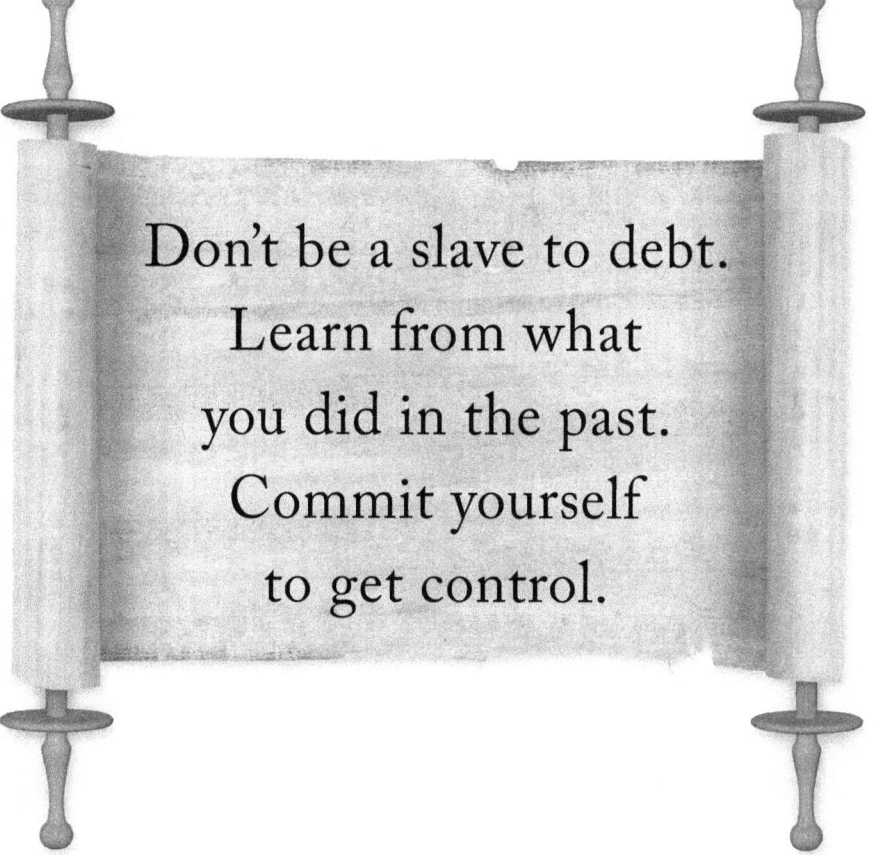

Don't be a slave to debt. Learn from what you did in the past. Commit yourself to get control.

Define SMART Money Goals

Getting control of your finances is, perhaps, the best way to be a good steward. After taking an honest look at your income and expenses and setting a manageable monthly budget, you need to move on to the next step—getting control of your finances.

DEFINE SMART MONEY GOALS

You must establish SMART (specific, measurable, achievable, related/relevant, and time framed) goals for yourself. For example, "My financial goal is to achieve $\underline{X}$ results by $\underline{Y}$ date with a total debt reduction amount of $\underline{Z}$ dollars." This example is specific, measurable, and achievable, related to your finances, and has a time frame. Next, prioritize your debts by itemizing household and living expenses. This topic will be covered in more detail later. (See Step Four: Paying Off Debt).

Step Three has wise words to put into action now! Once you have set your goals, the most important thing to do is acknowledge God's ownership (bodies, abilities, time, and material possessions). Step Three will not waste your time but will get right to the point: It is God who will give you the power and the determination to do the work necessary to get control of your finances. This step teaches you how to have the right attitude about debt; to determine which bills must be paid and when; to find ways to cut back on unnecessary expenses; to maintain your own money, checking account, and credit card account. If you decide to manage your finances jointly, be responsible and do what works for both. Don't fight every month about who's responsible for what when it comes to your finances. Choose not to be a slave to your debt; choose to get on the right path and stay on the right path. Wealth is a gift *from* God, and what we do with that wealth is our gift *to* God.

A BIBLICAL PRINCIPLE:
INSPIRATION TO HELP YOU MEET YOUR FINANCIAL GOALS

COMMITMENT TO THE LORD

Make a commitment to get control of your finances. Proverbs 16:3 NIV says: *"Commit to the Lord whatever you do, and your plans will succeed."*

> *Adoniram Judson, missionary to Burma, was born on August 9, 1788 in Malden, Massachusetts. After graduating from Brown University in 1809, he became a Christian. In February 1812, he set sail with his new bride for India where he soon discovered that country was closed to foreign missionaries.*

> *But he learned that Burma was open to foreign missionaries, so he made a commitment that he "would not leave Burma until the cross is planted here forever." It was six years before his first convert to Christianity, and ten years before he completely translated the New Testament into Burmese.*
>
> *Despite spending six months in prison on falsely being accused as a spy, and his wife becoming sick and having to return home to their homeland, he remained in Burma for 25 more years. "Life is short. Millions of Burmese are perishing. I am almost the only person on earth who has attained their language to communicate salvation", he wrote.*[4]

Adoniram Judson made a commitment that he would not leave Burma until a cross was planted there forever. He kept his commitment.

The message is this: Make a commitment to get control of your finances. Don't be a slave to debt. Learn from what you did in the past. Commit yourself to get control. *Finances & Spirituality* is a seven-step plan to help you achieve better success with your financial goals.

Your Money Matters
Discover How Your Money Could Be Doing More

ELIMINATE CREDIT CARD DEBT

The average credit card debt as of December 2012 was $7,117. This is the worst kind of debt you can have, but there is hope. You are not alone. The average household debt in 2012 was $15,257. It was higher for African-American families earning between $10,000 and $24,999 a year.[5]

Credit card debt is the worst kind of debt you can have. For Example - The payback time calculated on a credit card balance of $14,750 (assuming no additional purchases) will be 57.3 years based on an average interest rate of 18% and paying the credit card minimum monthly payment (2%). During this 57.3 year period, you will end up paying $42,649.09 in interest! The bottom line is this: The total payback will be $57,403.09 ($14,750 + $42,649.09). If you pay an extra $10 a month, you can repay the loan in fewer years and you will save yourself several thousand dollars in interest.

Those who love their credit cards prioritize in this way: Pay bills first, spend, and save last. After they pay bills, they spend at will what is left. Saving, if any, is the smallest share of their paycheck. *"In the house of the wise are stores of choice food and oil, but a foolish man devours all he has"* (Proverbs 21:20 NIV).

Those who serve God (Master) prioritize differently: They honor God first, save, pay bills, and then spend what is left.

In *Finances & Spirituality*, we encourage you to put first things first. After setting aside your tithe (God first!)–then save, pay bills, and anything leftover is for spending. Learn to put *first* things *first!*

> *Will a man rob God? Yet you rob me. But you ask, "How do we rob you?" "In tithes and offerings. You are under a curse –the whole nation of you—because you are robbing me. Bring the whole tithe into the storehouse, that there may be food in my house. Test me in this," says the LORD Almighty, "and see if I will not throw open the flood-gates of heaven and pour out so much blessing that you will not have room enough for it."* (Malachi 3:8-10 NIV)

It is time now to "shift" your wealth priorities. *"No one can serve two masters. Either he will hate the one and love the other, or he will be devoted to the one and despise the other. You cannot serve both God and money"* (Matthew 6:24 NIV). Are you trying to serve both?

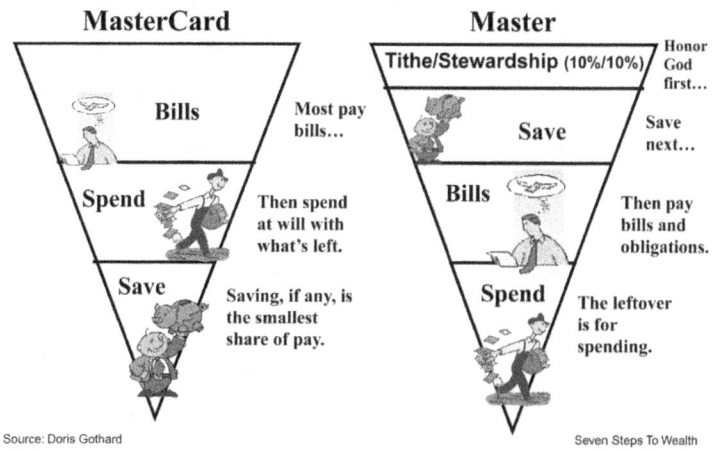

Be realistic about your credit card debt. Penalty fees add up. Late fees add up. Over-the-limit fees add up. Annual renewal fees add up. Does this mean we can't have debt? The answer is no! Just remember that payback is hard! Before making any purchases via your credit card, ask yourself if you really want to do this.

KNOW YOUR CREDIT SCORE

Your credit score can make or break your financial future. Most lenders use a measurement called a credit score to determine approval for a loan. It is a numerical expression of your creditworthiness. Credit scores are used to determine how much you pay for life's needs: mortgages, car loans, cell phones, apartment rentals, insurance, credit cards, etc. It is important to know the meaning of your credit score and be familiar with all three credit bureaus. There are three credit bureaus—Equifax, Experian, Trans-Union—and each publishes a credit score based on your credit history. Each may have a different overall credit score for you.

Your credit score says a lot about how you manage your finances. If you have been denied, you can most likely chalk it up to your credit score. The higher your credit score (740+), the lower your loan interest rate and you will pay fewer fees, if any. Know your credit score! All three credit bureaus have the following rankings for credit scores.

CREDIT SCORE RANKINGS

- 750 - 850+ = Superstar!
- 700 - 749 = Good
- 650 - 699 = Average
- 600 - 649 = Poor
- Below 600 = Deadbeat *(No loan!)*

GET FREE CREDIT REPORT UPDATES

Knowing your score is only part of the picture. You need to check to make sure that all of the information in each report is true and up to date. Be warned that each company might have different information! It can be a long process to get each report updated, but the results of such efforts can be very rewarding.

You can request a free copy of your credit report every 12 months from each of the major credit-reporting agencies - Equifax, Experian and TransUnion by visiting www.annualcreditreport.com. A couple of the agencies will send you free updates. For example, Credit Sesame will track your Experian credit report daily and Credit Karma will track your TransUnion report. Both services are free of charge. Free credit report tracking will give you an instant heads-up that there has been a change in your report and it will help you identify fraud quickly. Sign up for free Experian credit report monitoring with **CREDIT SESAME** (www.creditsesame.com/credit-monitoring), and TransUnion monitoring with Credit Karma (www.creditkarma.com/credit-monitoring). You may also obtain free copies of your credit report from each bureau by going to their websites: Equifax, www.equifax.com; Experian, www.creditexpert.com; and Trans-Union, www.transunion.com. Under federal law, bureaus must provide you with a free report if you think it contains an error as a result of fraud. If you don't qualify for a free report, you can purchase it. Your credit score may not be included in a *free credit report*. As a result, you may be required to pay extra to get your score.

CLEAN UP YOUR CREDIT REPORT

What sort of things do you need to do? You need to stay low, lighten up, and dump the trash from your credit report. First, stay low. Keep your balances below 50% of your credit limit. Be careful about moving balances from card to card to take advantage of low interest rates, as often times shuffling will trigger a credit inquiry. Next, lighten up. Get rid of unneeded credit cards because more than four cards can hurt your score. Too many cards give you too much access to credit. Too many inquiries over a six month period may count against your credit score. Finally, dump the trash. Periodically check your credit report for old information (bankruptcies, older than 7-year-old lawsuits, commingled accounts, etc.). Request Equifax, Experian, and Trans-Union to remove "old" negative information from your report.

It is a credit report myth that your income is not tied to your credit report. It is possible to have an excellent credit score of 850 even if you are unemployed. If you move around often, it does not affect your credit score. Finally, your age does not affect your credit score.

PUT MORE MONEY IN YOUR POCKET

There are many, many ways to save a dollar here, a dollar there. When you have established a budget, determine what cutbacks you may need to make. Review your bills. There are many ways to bring down your monthly costs by negotiating changes in plans or service providers.

- *Phone/cable television/internet.* Don't hesitate to switch. There's a whole new world of competition; many will offer you better deals than your current company to gain your business. When the limited time offers are up, call again. Most will offer you another day to stay with them.

- *Wireless cellular service.* Ask for special concessions.

- *Credit cards.* Pay on time and get the lowest interest rate you can.

- *Mortgages.* Lock in low interest rates when available. Consider refinancing if rates have lowered since your last agreement; you can reduce your monthly mortgage expense by doing so.

- *Rent.* Renegotiate your lease. If your lease is up, negotiate hard, or move.

- *Vehicles.* If you've got a car or van that needs frequent repairs or guzzles gas, consider getting a new one when interest rates are low.

- *Insurance.* Ask your agent to review all your policies. Don't just look at lowering premiums, but make certain you've got the appropriate coverage for your current needs.

- *Mailing.* Plan ahead. Mail or ship early for lowest rate.

Cutting a few dollars off any of your bills might not seem like much. However, a few dollars here and a few dollars there, and pretty soon you're talking about real money.

Another way to take control and get more of your own money back into your pocket is to reevaluate your tax deductions claimed. Most taxpayers can pump up their paychecks even more by putting an end to over withholding for Uncle Sam. Millions of Americans get tax refund checks—proof that too much tax was taken from their checks. The average tax refund in 2009 was a record: $3,036, up $266 from the same period a year earlier. Listed below is the Historical Average Tax Refund for years 2007 to 2012.6

In previous years, the average tax refund has been in the same range, with the average peaking for the 2009 tax year before slipping:

- Average 2012 Refund: $2,803
- Average 2011 Refund: $2,913
- Average 2010 Refund: $3,003
- Average 2009 Refund: $3,036
- Average 2008 Refund: $2,728
- Average 2007 Refund: $2,699

Don't celebrate receiving a big tax refund check. Nearly a quarter of the people earn under $25,000/year. If you are in that category, it may make sense to adjust your tax withholding. Why should you give Uncle Sam 25% of the money you could have had in your pocket all along? To stop overwithholding, file a new W-4 form with your employer. The more allowances you claim, the less tax will be withheld, and the more of your salary you'll get when you earn it.

WEALTH CHECK-UP

Manage your credit information responsibly. Credit Bureaus use the information they receive about your credit to determine your credit score. You boost your credit score by reviewing your credit information annually.

Which of the following best describes what you know about your credit report?

❏ I have never seen a copy of my credit report.

❏ I have seen my credit report but I did not understand it.

❏ I have seen my credit report and my credit record was poor.

❏ I have seen my credit report and my credit record was good.

If you receive more than $100 in your tax refund each year, you may want to readjust your deduction estimates to keep more of your money in your pocket throughout the year.

Which of the following best describes that your tax estimates are well targeted right now?

❏ I get less than $100 refund on my tax return.

❏ I get more than $100 refund on my tax return.

❏ I owe nothing at the end of the year on my tax return and I don't get anything back.

STEP FOUR: DO GOOD

Get out of debt. Spend less than you make and offer acts of financial kindness to others in need.

Perform Random Acts of Kindness

So far, we have taken three steps in *Finances & Spirituality*. In Step One, we got a better understanding of our reactions to money and we put our emotions in spiritual alignment. In Step Two, we worked on being honest about our income and spending and creating a budget. In Step Three, we discussed getting control by determining when to borrow and understanding our credit report and credit scores. You established SMART (specific, measurable, achievable, related/relevant, and time framed) goals in Step Three. In Step Four, we will examine ways to DO GOOD: DO Get Out Of Debt!

PERFORM RANDOM ACTS OF KINDNESS

Do you know you cannot perform random acts of financial kindness when you spend more than you make? Dealing with the burden of debt is a global issue. *USA Today* reported two years ago that nearly two thirds of twenty-somethings in America have some debt, and those with debt have taken on more in the past five years.[7] Last year in Australia, credit-reference company Veda Advantage revealed that 18- to 27-year-olds were responsible for a third of all defaults on credit obligations listed with the company. The figures also show that of the record 3.7 million new credit card applications in 2006, almost a third of those were from that same age group.[8]

In Step Four, you are encouraged to "do good" things – not to be seen but because you see needs and you are moved to make a difference. This kind of attitude will influence others to do the same. In order to get your finances back on track, you must first admit you have a problem that is out of control, and then you have to commit yourself to taking action. Once you have taken care of your own debt, you are free to "do good" things to help others.

The purpose of *Finances & Spirituality* is to give Biblical principles for correcting bad money habits: get out of debt, find release from debtors, and have enough left to respond to the financial needs of other people, no matter who or what is responsible for their condition. Today, many people are in debt, challenged by high gasoline prices, energy crisis, surging oil prices, mortgage crisis, and credit crisis. Some may feel that it is their own fault; however, there are reasons why people fall on hard times. We should not close our hearts and hands to those in need. I encourage you to "do good" things. If you find yourself arguing with your spouse, children or loved ones every month about money, stop fighting and work together. DO GOOD. Give something back! Perform random acts of financial kindness!

Doris Gothard

A BIBLICAL PRINCIPLE:
INSPIRATION TO HELP YOU MEET YOUR FINANCIAL GOALS

GIVING BACK

"Freely you have received, freely give" (Matthew 10:8 NIV).

> *Albert Lexie gets out of bed at 5 a.m. every Tuesday and Thursday, takes two buses to the Children's Hospital of Pittsburgh, and makes his rounds—offering shoestrings for $3. Every Tuesday, Lexie hands over his weekly donation to the hospital's Free Care Fund, which helps pay for pediatric patients' treatment. Lexie has donated more than $89,000 since 1981. "You know when Albert is in because everyone is walking around in their socks," said hospital spokeswoman Melanie Finnigan.* (Reader's Digest, December 2003, p. 36)

> *Every act of self-sacrifice for the good of others will strengthen the spirit of beneficence in the giver's heart, allying him more closely to the Redeemer of the world, who "was rich, yet for our sakes became poor, that we through His poverty might be rich." And it is only as we fulfill the divine purpose in our creation that life can be a blessing to us.*[9]

The real reason to get out of debt is to help yourself, your family, and others in need. The spirit of getting out of debt is not for the love of money. It is so that we can "do good." Romans 13:8 NIV says, *"Let no debt remain outstanding, except the continuing debt to love one another."* Give back. *"Each of you must bring a gift in proportion to the way the LORD your God has blessed you"* (Deuteronomy 16:17 NIV). *"Freely you have received, freely give"* (Matthew 10:8 NIV). To whom much is given, much is required.

The gift of wealth that God gives us carries great responsibilities. Let us do good by getting out of debt so that we may be rich in good works, ready to give, willing to share. God commands us to *"do good, to be rich in good deeds, and to be generous and willing to share"* (I Timothy 6:18 NIV). Jerry Thomas writes, "God's blessings come from human hands. He teaches us to see every person in need as a neighbor and see the world as our neighborhood."[10]

The message is this: To whom much is given much is required. Share freely with the poor. Pay down your debt—DO Get Out Of Debt!—and give back.

Your Money Matters
Discover How Your Money Could Be Doing More

MANAGE YOUR CREDIT

Credit is a tool that can help build wealth quickly. However, if too much credit is obtained, you can lose all your wealth. Using credit, or borrowing money you don't have, is not an advantage in the following circumstances:

- The interest rates are high, and the funds obtained are expensive.

- The asset purchased depreciates quickly leaving increased debt.

- You don't have enough income to make the payments and default on the loan.

No more than 25% of your gross monthly income should be used on installment debt. If there aren't sufficient funds to pay bills, contact your lender immediately. Late payments on bills can be very expensive. Paying bills late will have a negative effect on your credit score. The next time you ask to borrow funds, the lender will increase your interest rate, which will have a negative impact on your creditworthiness. When payments are late, there is a possibility you could lose your collateral or be sued. A bankruptcy will remain on your credit report for at least seven years if you are unable to pay your debts.

It is important your monthly debt payments do not exceed monthly income. The key is to not spend more than your income! Managing debt will put you in a better financial situation. There are two types of debt: unsecured debt and secured debt. Unsecured debt includes personal loans and credit card debt. Secured debt includes the mortgage and any home equity or car loans. Are you on track for increasing your cash and reducing your debt?

To get your finances back on track, take definite and committed steps with resiliency to eliminate debt. First, you must prioritize your debts by itemizing essential household and living expenses such as your house, utilities, and transportation to work, as addressed in the two previous steps. Then, create a plan to eliminate that debt.

PAYING OFF DEBT

The quickest way to pay-off your debt is to follow a plan:

1. Determine your current total debt payments and pay off the lowest balance accounts first to give yourself some incentive.

2. Sort your debts from highest interest rate to lowest.

3. Continue to make the same total payment amount but pay minimum payments on all debts except the highest interest rate debt.

4. On the highest interest rate account, pay the minimum payment + $10. Continue until the highest interest rate is paid off. Once the highest interest rate debt is paid off, apply those new savings to the next highest rate debt.

5. Start over!

To expedite the paying-off debt process, contact your creditors to negotiate a lower debt balance payoff or to explore bill paying options. Call each account. Ask: "Hi, I'm calling about my account. I see I'm paying a rate of (insert your rate). Is there any way I can lower that?" Probe. Don't take a simple "No" or "That's our standard rate" for an answer. Ask if they have rates available for new accounts or larger customers. Ask to have those rates applied to you. If the person you're speaking with says, "I do not have the authority to talk with you about adjusting your account," ask to speak to someone who has the authority. Negotiate. Since few customers take the time to call for better rates, most companies will offer you something. Take that as a starting point, not a final offer. Mention the other deals you've seen or been offered. Be courteous. The goal is to have vendors want to keep you as a customer. If you're belligerent, they'll be happy to see you go.

If you own a home, a home equity loan is one way to pay off credit card debt. This topic is discussed in more detail in Step Five. Sometimes you need outside help to assist you to Do GOOD. You can try beginning with a debt repayment plan with an accredited nonprofit credit-counseling agency. If you live on a low, fixed income, you should consult with a local legal aid office and learn your rights.

LEARN HOW TO STAND UP TO BILL COLLECTORS

Sometimes your bills are just too much. Perhaps this was due to "user error" on your part, or perhaps it was due to a job change/loss or the economy. No matter what the reason, you can still do something to help yourself work through your debt. Many bill collectors are willing to work with you if you learn to work with them and learn to work within the system.

The first thing you need to do is learn your rights as a consumer. Call the National Consumer Law Center for a free brochure – 617-542-9595. Armed with knowledge of your rights, call the customer service center for one of the creditors who has been badgering you. It is usually better to negotiate at the end of the month versus the beginning of the month. Stay calm and focused; keep your cool and concentrate on the negotiation process. Tape the call if you can, but only after checking the law in your state to determine if it is legal to tape telephone calls. At the very least, take notes. You need to make sure there's a record of your conversation. Record the date and time and the name/operator number of the person with whom you speak.

Once you are connected with a finance representative, be polite and cordial. Control the information flow; keep private information private and provide no personal information. Don't tell them your life story. Everyone has hardships. Instead, just estimate how much you can pay and offer less. Get proof of payment agreement in writing, and then send a letter to the debt collector outlining the payment agreement. Follow up by cleaning up your credit report. Ask debt collectors to remove any negative information they've placed on your credit report. Make sure you make these new payments on time to honor your agreement and avoid sending postdated checks.

STAYING OUT OF DEBT

Now that you know what your total debt regular bills are per month, start putting aside money each week to pay your regular monthly bills. Put more when you have extra. Get in the habit of writing down how much money you spend each day and how much money you have left each week. Open up two bank accounts, one for your daily transactions and another dedicated for a savings account. Shop around for a bank that offers the highest interest on a savings account and has minimum or no administrative charges. Automatically transfer a fixed amount of money from your daily transactions account to your savings account each month. Cut out all unnecessary spending. Know the difference between your needs and your wants. If it's something you feel you must have, save up for it; don't charge it or borrow money to get it. Use your credit card just like you would your debit card. Only charge what you will be able to pay when the credit card bill is received. Pay your credit card bill in full each month. Pay on time because the interest charges on late payments are extremely high. Don't be afraid to ask for professional financial advice if you need help. Jesus said, *"Ask and it will be given to you; seek and you will find; knock and the door will be opened to you. For everyone who asks receives; he who seeks finds; and to him who knocks, the door will be opened"* (Luke 11:9, 10 NIV).

GOOD DEBT

Not all debt is bad. Some debt is actually good. There are basically four types of good debt: house mortgage, loan for college, investment debt, and home equity debt. Good debt includes anything you need but can't afford to pay for up front without wiping out cash reserves or liquidating all your investments.

A *house mortgage* can be considered good debt because you can build equity in your home, and the mortgage interest and real estate taxes are tax deductible. You have the possibility of making some money when you sell your home or leave it to your heirs. However, low credit scores and the increased amount for a house mortgage down payment required by some lenders may be factors keeping people out of today's home buying market. During the housing boom, the median down payment for purchasing a home was about 15% and the average credit score required was about 720. In today's market, the median down payment has risen from 15% to 20%, and credit scores for Fannie Mae loans, Freddie Mac, and FHA have risen from 720 to 760. Loans made to borrowers with credit scores of 620 or below are almost nonexistent. A house mortgage can be considered good debt; however, these factors may be insurmountable obstacles for many young house hunters, thereby reducing the number of home buyers.

Consider *college loans* for the purposes of education as an investment (good debt). Though college loans will initially be a hardship, in the long run the increased income that goes along with a college degree will be a better investment. It has been said that it takes money to make money.

Investment debt may also be considered good debt. No one gets rich using only his/her own money. If you can borrow to make money, then do it. Sometimes when an investment opportunity arises, you have to choose to take on a little debt in pursuit of greater return.

A *home equity loan* is the fourth type of "good debt" if you are a homeowner. This topic will be discussed in more depth in Step Five.

WEALTH CHECK-UP

In Step Four, we examined ways to become debt-free. We examined ways to DO GOOD: DO Get Out Of Debt! We learned that money is a talent to be used and how to establish a plan for paying off the monthly bills as well as paying off any indebtedness as a result of debt.

Which of the following best describes your attitude about Getting Out Of Debt?

❑ I will stop acquiring new debt.

❑ I will not use my credit cards to borrow money.

❑ I will establish an emergency fund.

❑ I will implement a debt payoff plan.

❑ I will designate a certain amount of money to pay toward debts each month.

❑ I will prioritize my debts from highest interest rate to lowest.

- ❏ I will pay off the lowest balance account first to give myself some incentive and I will throw all I can at the debt with the next-lowest balance.

- ❏ I will pay the minimum monthly payment on all debts except for the one with the highest interest rate where an additional $10 will be added to the minimum monthly payment until the debt is paid off.

- ❏ When that debt is gone, I will not alter the monthly amount used to pay my debts.

- ❏ I will pay my credit card bills on time each month to create a positive effect on my credit report.

STEP FIVE: PAY FOR YOUR FUTURE

Build your wealth through savings and investments and provide a good life for yourself and your family.

Build a Nest Egg Through Savings and Investments

AFTER YOU HAVE CHECKED YOUR emotions, put them in spiritual alignment, gotten control of your finances and worked to Get Out Of Debt, it is time for Step Five—PAY FOR YOUR FUTURE by building your wealth through savings and investments.

BUILD WEALTH THROUGH SAVINGS AND INVESTMENTS

Growing your savings over time is key to your future. *"In the house of the wise are stores of choice food and oil, but a foolish man devours all he has"* (Proverbs 21:20 NIV).

Take charge of your finances and begin to save more. If you lost your job, how long could you live off your savings? Make saving a priority! Use direct deposit to automate a savings plan.

Learn to kick your most costly emotional behavior. It's called overspending! When you change your relationship with the things you love to buy, you will save more. Here are some tips to kick the habit.

TIPS TO STOP OVERSPENDING

Don't Touch. Don't pick up that $150 pair of new shoes because it will increase your desire to buy it. Touching the shoes makes it more difficult for you to resist buying.

Ask yourself. Ask yourself: : "Do I really need to spend $150 on another pair of shoes?" The answer is probably not. Try saving the money for a trip to Hawaii.

Make it harder. Shop with a list, set a target, and pay cash for purchases. Mentally ballpark your spending while you shop. Stick to your target.

Push yourself. Push yourself to save, no matter what. Save systematically!

In *Finances & Spirituality*, we acknowledge God's ownership, honor Him with the first 10% of our income (tithe), then save, and pay bills. This is what God requires. *"A tithe of everything from the land, whether grain from the soil or fruit from the trees, belongs to the LORD; it is holy to the LORD"* (Leviticus 27:30 NIV). The remaining 90% of our income is what God allows us to use as we please (give a love offering to God, save, pay bills, help others, etc.). Wealth is God's gift to you; what you do with that wealth is your gift to God.

A BIBLICAL PRINCIPLE:
INSPIRATION TO HELP YOU MEET YOUR FINANCIAL GOALS

HOLY TO THE LORD

"A tithe of everything from the land, whether grain from the soil or fruit from the trees, belongs to the LORD; it is holy to the LORD" (Leviticus 27:30 NIV).

> *W. A. Criswell tells of an ambitious young man who told his pastor he'd promised God a tithe of his income. They prayed for God to bless his career. At that time he was making $40.00 per week and tithing $4.00. In a few years his income had increased and he was tithing $500.00 per week. He called the pastor to see if he could be released from his tithing promise, as it was too costly.*

The pastor replied, "I don't see how you can be released from your promise, but we can ask God to reduce your income to $40.00 a week, then you'll have no problem tithing $4.00." (W. A. Criswell, <u>A Guidebook for Pastors</u>, p. 156)

God has promised that he will bless the conscientious person who returns a faithful tithe (Malachi 3:8-10). Only those who have experienced the goodness of the Lord by faithfully tithing can fully appreciate this spiritual truth. "Test me in this,' says the Lord Almighty" (Malachi 3:10).[11]

Have you heard the expression, "It's not how much money you make; it's what you do with what you make"? Commit everything to the Lord, and you will receive a wealthy treasure, a gift from God that will give you financial success that will last forever. *"Now to him who is able to do immeasurably more than all we ask or imagine, according to his power that is at work within us"* (Ephesians 3:20 NIV).

The message is this: The Lord will make you successful in everything you do when your delight is in Him. Pray for the day when you will no longer have debt which prevents you from being able to **save** a little, help yourself, your family, and others.

Your Money Matters
Discover How Your Money Could Be Doing More

MAKE SAVING A PRIORITY

Is saving money important? Yes, more so now than ever before. Saving can transform your future. However, most people have a spending problem, not a savings problem. They live paycheck to paycheck. They're broke. The money they spend on "little stuff" (manicures, salons, eating out, etc.) really adds up. Just think what cutting out a few of these extras could mean for you financially. Cancel cable. No more Starbucks. If you spend more than you make, you can't save or invest. Wealth does not happen by accident. It takes time and planning, good decision-making, patience, and discipline based on properly set priorities. *"Plans fail for lack of counsel, but with many advisers they succeed"* (Proverbs 15:22 NIV). To achieve wealth, you need to live on a budget and purposefully budget to save some of your money in order for your money to grow. If you work overtime hours, save the income from your overtime pay. The longer you save, the bigger your growth; therefore, the sooner you start saving, the better.

You have already learned that your money will not grow in a piggy bank. You need to find a place to invest your savings. When you use your money to make more money, it's called investing. The original amount you saved is called capital. The amount added to it by investing is called growth.

Your money makes money when you buy something today that may be worth more tomorrow after selling it. There are both risks and rewards to making money. It is important to know that sometimes when you invest an original amount of money (capital), you can lose your money. No matter how you look at it, it hurts to lose. You should never invest what you cannot afford to lose. Have a plan to manage your finances. Save. Protect your future! Only start investing after you build an emergency savings account to avoid using your investments for monthly emergencies. If you want to invest in stocks, bonds, mutual funds, and annuities, educate yourself first by reading financial magazines such as Money, Kiplinger, etc. Next, consult with your bank or an experienced financial advisor.

Don't forget that to provide the resources for you and your family to live a good life, you must pay for your future by setting up a budget and savings plan. It takes very little money to make money when you develop a budget and follow it. If you get money and budget to save it, you will see your money grow. You don't need a lot to start with. Many investments can be made with just $25. Even without earning, finding, winning, borrowing, or getting money as a gift, you can end up with more money if you are patient and consistent in your journey toward financial wealth.

Building your wealth doesn't mean winning the lottery. Most people build wealth the old-fashioned way: They SAVE over time. When investing, you should plan for the long term because money markets go up and down over short terms. But, historically, they grow over the long term. Start simply. Find a way to save $5 to $10 a day. It's not glamorous, but SAVING is important. There are many places that offer free savings strategies. For example, at the America Saves website (http://www.americasaves.org), you can read various articles related to your specific financial situation, access the American Saver Newsletter, view fact sheets on different ways to save, and gain a free financial education. You can get lots of additional information on a variety of the topics covered in this book including information on understanding your credit score and needs and various types of insurance and investments at the Federal Citizen Information Center (www.pueblo.gsa.gov). However, be a good steward by wisely and carefully investing money.

MAKE SAVING A PRIORITY

Before you can save, you need to have followed Steps One through Five of this book. You first need to create a budget, pay down bills, and practice good credit card management. Learn to live below your means. You should also establish a rainy day fund before making long-term investments. Invest a portion of your after-tax income to an additional savings account (10% to 15% to a rainy day fund) over and above your retirement savings.

Most people take their hard-earned paycheck and pay everyone else first. They pay the car loan, mortgage, utility bill, cell phone bill, etc. *Pay yourself first!*

On June 7, 2001, President George W. Bush signed into law a massive new tax reform bill known as the Economic Growth and Tax Relief Reconciliation Act of 2001. You can now put significantly more money than ever before into tax-deductible and tax-deferred retirement accounts. Some of the ways you can make your money work for you are to get a money market checking account, invest in a pretax retirement account such as a 401(k), 403(b), IRA, annuities, or invest in stocks or mutual funds, or invest in property.

MONEY MARKET ACCOUNTS

The richest 1% of Americans save 20% of their income. If you want to be among the 1%, save 20%! The key to any savings plan is to save systematically. Get a *money market checking account*. It pays a higher interest rate versus a regular checking or savings account. However, during the battered down economy in 2010, *money market checking account* interest return rates dropped to an all time low. But, I encourage you to save a cushion of funds in a money market checking account rather than a regular checking account. Keep enough in a savings account or money market checking account to cover at least six to eight months of your monthly expenses.

When you save your money in an interest-bearing account, interest is added to your savings. This doesn't happen when your money is held in a piggy bank or under a mattress. Find a way to save a little each month. You will be surprised at the results.

It is not a big deal to save if you do it through payroll deductions or direct deposits to an Interest-bearing account. It is a way to save money and earn income on your savings. Currently, 2013 money market savings account rates are less than 1%. However, earning some interest is better than earning no-interest on your money.

To build your wealth, pay yourself first, and do it monthly. You can do it! Remember, to make your savings work for you, save at least $5.00 a day! "All hard work brings a profit, but mere talk leads only to poverty" (Proverbs 14:23 NIV).

The chart below was created to show what the estimated money savings can do for you when you save systematically. The chart shows earnings before the battered economy in 2010, when the interest-bearing account rates of return ranged from 4% to a high of 9%. Take a look at the chart.

Your Monthly Investment	Your Age	Total Amount Of Monthly Investments Through Age 65	At A 4% Rate Of Return	At A 7% Rate Of Return	At A 9% Rate Of Return	At A 12% Rate Of Return
$100	25	48,000	118,433	263,264	469,865	1,182,172
	30	42,000	91,543	180,588	295,147	645,839
	40	30,000	51,494	81,179	112,677	188,761
	50	18,000	24,642	31,748	37,910	50,066
$150	25	72,000	177,650	394,896	707,398	1,773,258
	30	63,000	137,315	270,883	442,721	968,758
	40	45,000	77,242	121,768	168,592	282,717
	50	27,000	36,963	47,621	56,865	75,099
$200	25	96,000	236,867	526,529	939,731	2,364,345
	30	84,000	183,086	361,177	590,294	1,291,678
	40	60,000	102,989	162,358	224,789	376,957
	50	36,000	49,289	63,495	75,819	100,132

PRETAX RETIREMENT ACCOUNTS ARE A GREAT WAY TO SAVE

You may be wondering, why talk about a pretax retirement account? Don't let the name "pretax" scare you because a pretax retirement account is a great way to SAVE. It was named after a section in the Internal Revenue Code. Retirement saving is important, and you should take advantage of every retirement savings plan available to you through your employer. Plans offered may vary, but check with your employer.

To help you better understand the importance of building your wealth through savings and investments so you and your family can live a comfortable life in retirement, I have created a Stages of Life Chart to show you the percent of time in a lifetime (estimate of 86 years) you will likely spend in retirement – 20 years, second only to 40 years working life cycle. See chart below.

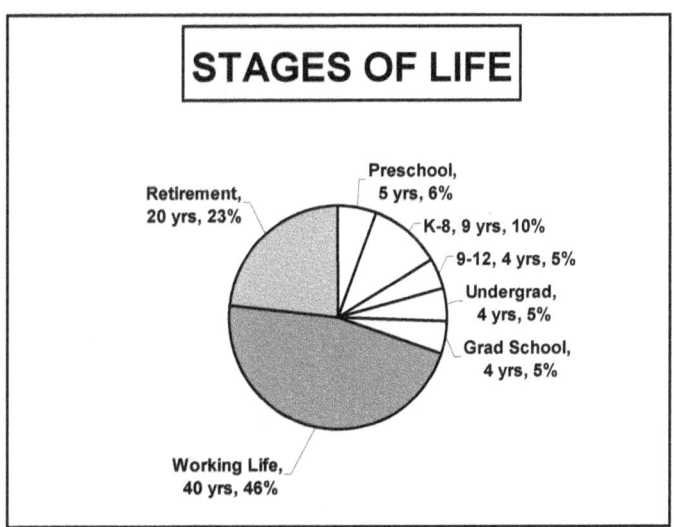

What does that mean for you? It means you will need to SAVE more now to be prepared for your retirement years—the years where you are not guaranteed any income unless you plan ahead. It is likely that Social Security will not provide you with enough income to maintain your current lifestyle. You may think about investing your retirement savings in a riskier investment plan when you're young and lean toward safer investments when you are older.

To help you guesstimate how to invest your retirement savings – See charts below.

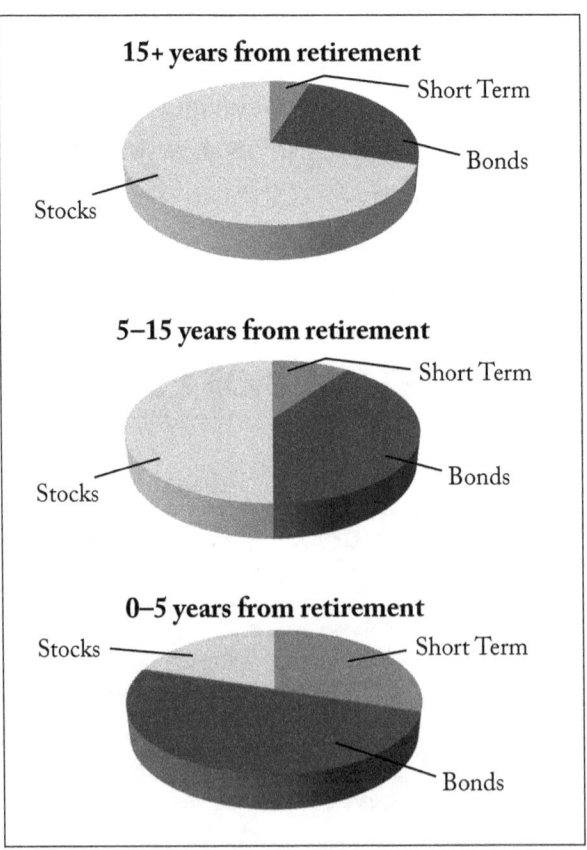

Ask your employer if your company offers a pretax retirement plan. It will allow you to make pre-tax contributions through payroll deductions, and you do not pay any income tax on the money that is deferred into the plan. The money that you save in the plan can earn interest and continue to grow tax-deferred. Two such accounts are 403(b) and 401(k) accounts.

A 403(b) is a pre-tax retirement account for those who work for schools, hospitals, or local government agencies. It allows you to invest money for retirement in a number of ways, including mutual funds. A 401(k) is a pre-tax retirement account that allows you to invest money for retirement in a number of ways. These may include mutual funds that invest in stocks, bonds or money markets, annuities or guaranteed investment pools, company stocks, or even self-directed brokerage accounts. Most plans offer a selection of various investment options that will allow you to create a suitable retirement portfolio. Money can generally be withdrawn from a 401(k) on five different occasions: termination of employment, disability, reaching age 59½ (or 55 in some cases), retirement, and death.

It is important to note that in some cases if money is withdrawn from these accounts before reaching age 59½, the IRS will issue a 10% early withdrawal penalty. Outside of the five qualified distribution events, you may be able to access a portion of your money if your plan allows loans. If you withdraw money, you will only be taxed on the money you withdraw from the plan. The table below shows what saving money systematically in a 401(k) savings plan can do for you:

$6000 in a 401(k)

Year	401(k)	Interest Earned (8%)
1	$ 6,000	$ 480
2	6,000	996
3	6,000	1,558
4	6,000	2,163
5	6,000	2,816
6	6,000	3,521
7	6,000	4,283
8	6,000	5,106
9	6,000	5,993

In the example above, if you invest $6,000 in your 401(k) and leave it there for nine years, it will earn interest each year. At the end of the nine-year period, you will have grown your money by $5,994. Your total funds after nine years = $6,000 + $5,994 = $11,994. It is important, however, to only invest money you know you can afford to leave for 8-10 years.

Unless it is absolutely necessary, do not to borrow from your 401(k). If you borrow from your 401(k), you may have terms and conditions that make the loan unattractive. In addition, it can seriously impact the long-term value of your retirement account, even if the loan is repaid after just a few years. When people are in a pinch for cash, their first thought is to borrow from their 401(k) retirement plan, often because borrowing from the plan appears to have advantages over traditional bank loans. Use a calculator to determine financial impact before you borrow. The Credit Union National Association at http://hffo.cuna.org offers an online calculator. The calculator not only shows the cost of borrowing the money but also calculates what that money would have helped you earn years down the road had you left it in place in your retirement account over the life of the loan.

If you borrow from your 401(k), you will be subject to income tax. If you borrow from your 401(k), you will give up potential growth and you will have double taxation on pay back. In addition, you will have no tax savings. Borrowing from your 40l(k) should only be done as your last resort if it is absolutely the only place you can get the money you need.

STOCKS AND MUTUAL FUNDS

A *stock* is a certificate that shows that you own a small fraction of a corporation. Stocks are units or shares of ownership in a company. When you buy a stock, you are paying for a small percentage of the business. The most popular types of stock are common stocks and preferred stocks. A *common stock* is a security that represents ownership in a corporation. Owners of common stocks have rights to a company's assets only after bondholders, preferred shareholders, and other debt holders have been paid in full. A *preferred stock* has a higher claim on the assets and earnings than common stock. Preferred stock generally has a dividend that must be paid out before dividends to common stockholders, and the shares usually do not have voting rights. Stocks offering dividends that are higher than average are called *income stocks*. Stocks of companies that pay little or no dividends because the companies are reinvesting all their profits to grow are called growth stocks.

A *mutual fund* is a pool of money that is professionally managed for the benefit of all shareholders. When you invest in a mutual fund, you and a lot of other people put money into a collection. The mutual fund manager decides which stocks, bonds, and other investments to purchase with the money from the collection. Everyone who owns a piece of or share in the mutual fund gets to share in the profits—or the losses. By investing in a mutual fund, you can own stocks in more kinds of industries than you could on your own. You get diversification in your investment. There are many types of mutual funds. Some invest in only one area (technology, medicine, etc.). Others invest in international companies or companies that protect the environment. There are mutual funds for almost every type of investor you can imagine. Mutual funds are often listed in the financial pages of the newspapers. Some major companies are Fidelity, Vanguard, and Dreyfus.

The objective of investing is to provide the resources that can be used to buy a house, pay for a college education, and keep you and your family comfortable during your retirement. Before you invest in a mutual fund, consult with a financial planner. Read financial planning books. If you are skilled at using the Internet, it is very important to do some kind of online research. If you are interested in stocks, look at how well the fund manager has done in the past. Look at what kinds of companies the selected fund invests in. You can go to several online sites and review everything from stocks and bonds to mutual funds and learn a lot about overall financial planning. Morningstar and Quicken have websites offering free online financial tools (www.morningstar.com or www.quicken.com). Each website provides free access to reports, offering objective guidance to help you reach your investment goals.

Whether you decide to make your own stock/bond purchases, let an investment firm do it for you, or take the advice of a bank investment advisor in your selections, it is important to understand some basic investment strategies: conservative, balanced, growth, and aggressive growth.

The *conservative portfolio* approach has income and capital appreciation as its objective. This strategy may be appropriate for investors who want to preserve their capital and minimum fluctuations in market value. It might include a ratio of 20% stocks, 50% bonds, and 30% short-term investments.

A *balanced portfolio* aims for capital appreciation and income, an appropriate strategy for investors who want the potential for capital appreciation and some growth and who can handle some moderate fluctuations in market value. It might include a ratio of 50% stocks, 40% bonds, and 10% short-term investments.

A *growth portfolio* is one that aims to grow. This is the approach for investors who can withstand significant fluctuations in market value in the search for a strong return on investments. The portfolio might include a ratio of 70% stocks, 25% bonds, and 5% short-term investments.

Finally, an *aggressive growth portfolio* also aims to grow, but it is appropriate for investors who not only seek intense growth but who can also tolerate wide fluctuations in market values, especially over the short term. It might include a ratio of 85% stocks and 15% bonds.

If you choose to buy your own stock directly instead of through a mutual fund, you have more direct control over your capital investment. However, it is often difficult deciding when to sell or buy a stock. The important thing is to keep track of all your investments. Periodically check the price per share. You might want to take action if the price of your stock changes. This is the hard part. Many people believe that buying stock is simple compared to knowing when to sell. If the price of one of your stock goes down, you may want to sell it so that you don't lose any more money. On the other hand, you may actually want to buy more!

Investing a fixed dollar amount to purchase shares of stock over a long period of time, regardless of the price/share, is called dollar cost averaging. As an example, you buy 20 shares of IBM stock at $80/share for a total cost of $1,600. IBM stock drops to $60. You know the company is still solid and will rebound. You buy 20 more shares at $60 (total cost of $1,200). Now, you own 40 shares, having paid $2,800 ($1,600 + $1,200). Even though you bought some shares for $80, you will still make a profit if the stock goes back up from $60 to $75 because you bought it at an average price of $70!

HOME/PROPERTY OWNERSHIP

Many consumers are delaying big-ticket purchases indefinitely as the economy continues to sputter. If you want to buy a new home, no problem! That is, it should be no problem to buy a new home IF… you have no credit card debt, are spending less than you make, have a six months emergency fund, have a regular savings plan, and have income you can count on.

Most people build-up their wealth through home equity and tax benefits by becoming homeowners. Franklin D. Raines, former CEO, Fannie Mae Corporation is reported to have said, "One of the most important things you can do for your future is to become a homeowner. It is the basis for wealth for most Americans." If becoming a homeowner is important to you, try postponing your urge to purchase a car for the next two to three years while you save for your new house. If you want to become a homeowner in the future, take the following steps now:

1. Have a budget and practice good credit card management.

2. Pay off loans and credit cards.

3. Request negative comments to be removed from your credit report.

4. Make savings a priority.

5. Build an emergency fund by having a cash cushion worth six months of expenses.

When it is time to house shop, know your credit score. Get preapproved by a mortgage lender. Know what you can afford. Buy what you can afford—not more than you can afford. Do whatever it takes to protect your future.

If you own your own home and you want to sell your home and purchase a new home, it is important to know the amount of equity in your current home. The loan-to-value (LTV) is the ratio of your home loan amount to the value of your property. This ratio tells a lender how much equity you will have in your home. The higher your equity and the lower your LTV, the larger your stake in the investment and the less risk there is for the lender. An LTV of 80%, for example, means that you are putting 20% down and borrowing 80% of the property's value. Borrowers with less than 20% equity generally are required to buy private mortgage insurance (PMI), which protects the lender in case of a loan default. The borrower's circumstances and the type of loan determine LTV guidelines.

STEPS TO CREATING AN INVESTMENT PROGRAM

Always remember that the objective for investment is to provide the resources needed for yourself and your family to live a good life. Wealthy people who spend more than they make are no longer wealthy. Wealthy people manage their finances! They know how much they have left after subtracting all debts from their income. They know their net worth. You can too! But, remember, your income is not an asset. Your assets are equity in your home, bank savings and checking accounts, mutual funds, IRAs, 403(b), 401(k), federal payroll savings, car (Blue Book value), etc. Your liabilities are your car loan, credit card debt, mortgage, etc.

The steps below show what you can do to create an investment program to build your own wealth.

1. Calculate your *net worth* (the value of all your assets minus the total of all your liabilities). Review it periodically to determine your progress. Your net worth tells you...

    - How much you are worth.
    - How much you have left after you subtract all of your liabilities from all of your assets.
    - The value of your estate.
    - How well your investments are performing.

    Example:
    Total Assets = $57,650
    Total Liabilities: Car Loan ($19,800), Credit Card ($500) = $20,300
    Total Assets ($57,650) *minus* Total Liabilities ($20,300) = $37,350 (Net Worth!)

2. Establish a budget. Record all your expenses for a few months to verify your budget.

3. Accumulate three to six months of emergency savings. Money market accounts are best to use for this.

4. Eliminate credit card debt and other bad debts such as high interest loans. Your future savings won't get you anywhere if you're paying high interest on your debts.

5. Educate yourself by doing research on potential investments and reading financial articles (*Money Magazine, Kiplinger's Financial Magazine, Forbes, Bloomberg, Business Week*, newspaper financial section, *Black Enterprise*, or Internet websites such as Vanguard, Fidelity, USA Today, or Morningstar).

6. Write your financial goals.

7. Meet with a financial advisor, if necessary. Some banks provide free services.

8. Participate in your employer's pre-tax investment plan (401k, 403b, etc.) immediately. Sacrifice if you have to. But, remember to be a good steward by wisely and carefully investing your money.

Accumulation of money or material possessions is not good or bad in itself. However, ask yourself, do I control my desire for money, or does it control me? Ask yourself, do I spend within my budget? Ask yourself, how should I invest my retirement savings? Ask yourself, will I have enough to retire on?

WEALTH CHECK-UP

Place an "x" by the statements which best describe your financial situation.

1. Overall, my personal financial situation and my ability to PAY my bills, is secure.

    ❑ I strongly disagree   ❑ I agree
    ❑ I disagree   ❑ I strongly agree
    ❑ I somewhat agree

2. I find it easy to PAY my monthly bills from my current income:

    ❑ I strongly disagree   ❑ I agree
    ❑ I disagree   ❑ I strongly agree
    ❑ I somewhat agree

3. In addition to my savings plan, I have an emergency fund to cover expenses for a period of

    ❑ Zero months   ❑ Three months
    ❑ One month   ❑ Six or more months
    ❑ Two months

Place an "x" by the statements which best describe your "risk level" for investing your money.

1. If I had money to invest, I would invest in stocks or mutual funds for a period of:

   ❑ Less than 1-year   ❑ 5-9 years
   ❑ 1-2 years   ❑ 10 years or more
   ❑ 3-4 years

2. When it comes to investing in stocks or mutual funds, I would describe myself as a

   ❑ Very inexperienced investor
   ❑ Experienced investor
   ❑ Somewhat inexperienced investor
   ❑ Very experienced investor
   ❑ Somewhat experienced investor

3. I would be comfortable with investments that *lose* money from time to time – even if they offer the potential for *higher* returns.

   ❑ I strongly disagree   ❑ I agree
   ❑ I disagree   ❑ I strongly agree
   ❑ I somewhat agree

4. If I had money to invest, I would still keep an investment even if it *loses* 10% of its value over the course of a year.

   ❏ I strongly disagree ❏ I agree
   ❏ I disagree ❏ I strongly agree
   ❏ I somewhat agree

Write Your Investment Objective:

_____

_____

_____

_____

Example: My investment objective is to have a savings plan to save enough money to live comfortable during retirement and perhaps to leave a gift in my will or trust for my children.

STEP SIX: BE RESPONSIBLE

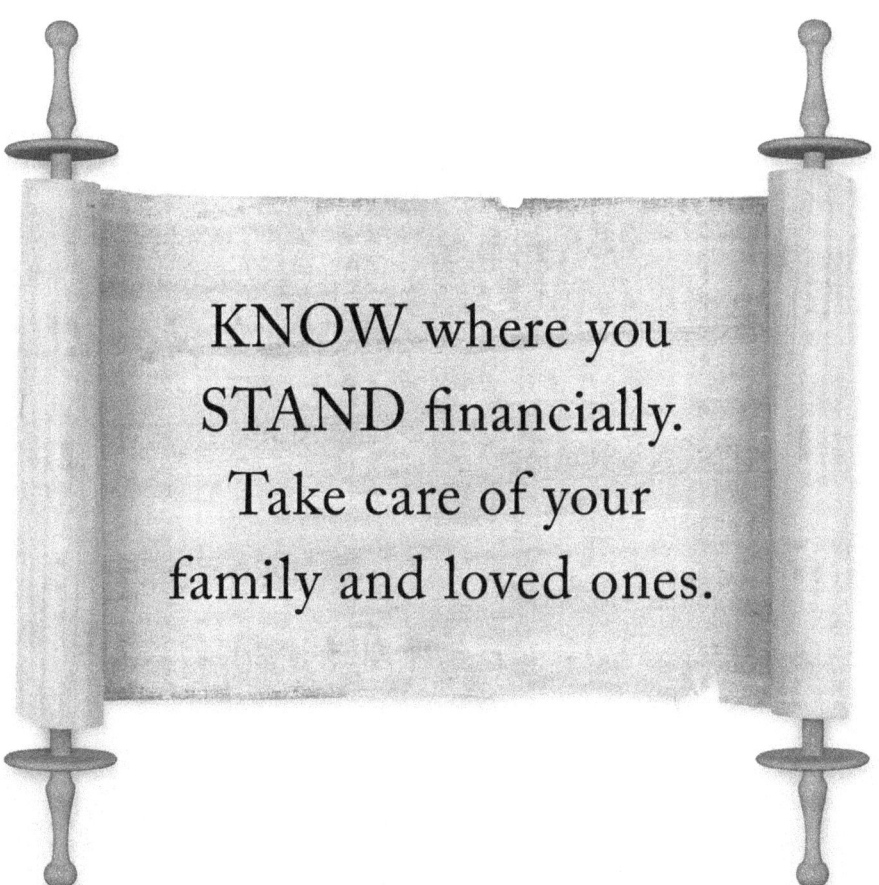

KNOW where you STAND financially. Take care of your family and loved ones.

KNOW WHERE YOU STAND AND TAKE CARE OF YOUR FAMILY AND LOVED ONES

WHEN YOU KNOW WHERE YOU STAND financially, you can't blame anyone else for your situation. Be responsible. Think about your family. Get life insurance. Get disability insurance.

TAKE CARE OF YOUR FAMILY AND LOVED ONES

If you really love your family, you will not only say you love them, but your actions will show it. Get a will or trust. Tomorrow is not promised. There are only two things that are certain along this journey to wealth—death and taxes. *"Give everyone what you owe him: If you owe taxes, pay taxes; if revenue, then revenue; if respect, if honor, then honor"* (Romans 13:7 NIV). Give your loved ones the care that they need before you die. Every state has tax laws regarding death. Each state and the District of Columbia taxes the transfer of assets after death. An asset is any item of economic value owned by an individual or corporation, especially that which could be converted to cash. Don't procrastinate. Create a will or a trust, but don't try to draft it at home by yourself. Start the process with an attorney and see it through. Don't hide your documents; tell a trusted loved one where the papers are. Update your will and trust regularly because circumstances in life change. Step Six: Be Responsible is about taking care of your family and loved ones. *"If anyone does not provide for his relatives, and especially for his immediate family, he has denied the faith and is worse than an unbeliever"* (1 Timothy 5:8 NIV). Being accountable and responsible for our finances is a non-negotiable standard.

A BIBLICAL PRINCIPLE:
INSPIRATION TO HELP YOU MEET YOUR FINANCIAL GOALS

NON-NEGOTIABLE STANDARDS

"*The earth is the Lord's, and everything in it, the world, and all who live in it; for he founded it upon the seas and established it upon the waters*" (Psalm 24:1-2 NIV).

> *Kirk Nowery, Executive Vice President of INJOY Stewardship Services, once penned The Seven Non-Negotiables of Stewardship, which are as follows:*
>
> 1. *God owns everything.*
>
> 2. *God's work must be supported by God's people.*

3. *God holds every person accountable.*

4. *God's will is that we give wisely and generously.*

5. *God desires equal commitment, not equal contribution.*

6. *God holds more responsible those to whom more is given.*

7. *God blesses the giver in a proportionate measure.*

About these seven non-negotiables, he comments, "God does not need anything; yet mysteriously, He wants us to grow in grace by giving to Him. As we obey Him in practicing this spiritual discipline, He blesses us accordingly. Jesus said, 'Give, and it will be given to you in return.' I urge you to etch these 'non-negotiables' into your own mind and heart."[12]

God holds more responsible those to whom much is given! God holds every person accountable. Those who are responsible with their money bless others and themselves at the same time. It's now time to be responsible. "*The Lord will lead you…You will be like a garden that has much water, like a spring that never runs dry*" (Isaiah 58:11 KJV).

DILIGENT HANDS BRING WEALTH

Every time we work to help another person, we help ourselves. *"Lazy hands make a man poor, but diligent hands bring wealth"* (Proverbs 10:4 NIV). When we take responsibility to give money or time to help another person, we help ourselves and those around us. The small acts of love and self-sacrifice that flow out from a life as quietly as the fragrance from a flower are the source of much of the blessings in life.

The message is this: Be responsible. Take care of your finances. Take care of your family. Make sure you know things are in order. Don't blame anyone else for your situation. It is your moral and social responsibility to be responsible!

Your Money Matters
Discover How Your Money Could Be Doing More

BE ACCOUNTABLE

You can delegate responsibility, but you can't delegate accountability. You can borrow for a college loan, but you cannot take out a loan for your retirement.

THE FOUR P'S OF RESPONSIBILITY

The sooner you start being responsible, the better. The "Four Ps" of responsibility are passion, priority, planning, and perseverance.

- o *Passion.* What are you passionate about? What do you really care about? Whatever you are passionate about will unlock the secret to finding your financial independence.

- *Priority.* Know where you stand financially, and know where you want to be. Remember, what you prioritize as most important will unlock the secret to finding your financial freedom.

- *Planning.* The reason is simple: the objective for having a financial plan is to provide the resources for you and your family to live a good life. Get health insurance. Get life insurance. Get a will and trust. Be responsible for those you love.

- *Perseverance.* At some point in your life you will want to purchase and pay for a house, pay for a college education, and keep you and your family comfortable in retirement. Are you tough enough to be responsible for those you love? Resilience and the ability to be responsible will ensure success for you and your family to live a comfortable life and extend a hand of financial kindness to those in need.

BE ACCOUNTABLE & RESPONSIBLE

Accountability	Responsibility
• **Know** where you STAND financially.	• **DON'T BLAME** anyone else for your situation.

Being accountable and responsible means knowing what you need to take care of for yourself and your family and not blaming anyone else for your situation. Some of the things you need to take care of include a will and/or trust, health insurance, life insurance, and disability and long-term care insurance.

Take care of your finances. Take care of your family. Make sure you know things are in order. Don't blame anyone else for your situation. It is your moral and social responsibility to be *responsible!*

DO YOU HAVE ENOUGH FOR RETIREMENT?

Keep saving for retirement before you actually go on retirement. You can take out a loan for college but you can't for retirement. Here is a chart to help guesstimate your retirement needs.

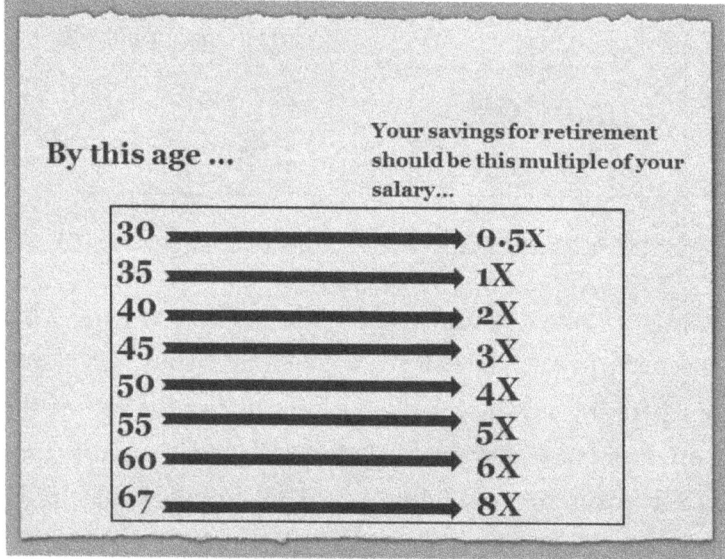

You must know where you stand financially before you retire. Once you know where you stand, you must take full responsibility to save for your retirement.

LIVING TRUSTS AND WILLS

There are people who think they don't need a will because they don't have anything of worth. This is far from the truth. Everyone has assets (your home, your car, your investment accounts, etc.). What happens to your property when you die? What happens if both you and your spouse die at the same time? What happens if one of you becomes sick or disabled? What happens to small children? Face the reality of your death. Protect your assets (your home, your car, your investment accounts, etc.) with a will or trust. You need both. Don't try to write them yourself because probate law is tricky; it varies from state to state. Find a good attorney who specializes in wills and trusts. Show your family how much you love them by making certain you have made provisions for them.

You must have a will or trust. A revocable living trust is a document stating who controls your assets (your house, your car, your investment accounts, etc.) while you are alive, and it designates who should be given those assets after you die. By naming yourself as the trustee of your trust, you control your assets as long as you live. Everything except your retirement accounts should be moved into a trust. The person who manages the assets in the trust is called a trustee. There are no probate (administrative) fees with a trust. There are, however, probate fees with a will. A will says where you want your assets to go but does not guarantee your assets will go where you intended. Remember to change your beneficiary designations if there is a change in your status. A trust is recommended because no one wants assets intended for loved ones used instead to pay the high cost of probate fees. Some families have been torn apart because of money issues arising from the death of a family member.

Let's take a look at two different situations. The mother of a family dies and has a will. If everything is left to children through her will, they must go through probate. Probate fees are based upon the total amount of the estate. Probate fees and legal fees must be paid when there is a will. When it comes to death, thousands of dollars can easily rack up in state-imposed death taxes, federal estate taxes, legal fees, and probate fees.

In the second situation, the mother dies and has a revocable living trust. There are no probate fees when you have a revocable living trust. Everything is left to her children via her trust. The trust bypasses the estate and is not included in the probate process. However, if the net worth of the estate is greater than $2 million, federal estate taxes must be paid.

> *While we know what the federal estate tax rules will be in 2010, 2011, and 2012, what will happen beyond 2012 is up in the air. Under current law the estate tax exemption is scheduled to drop significantly from $5,000,000 to $1,000,000 and the estate tax rate is scheduled to jump from 35% to 55% effective January 1, 2012. That's right – while the federal estate tax exemption has been set at $5,000,000 and the estate tax rate has been set at 35% for the 2010, 2011 and 2012 tax years,*

> *on January 1, 2013 the exemption and rate are scheduled to revert back to the numbers that were in effect in 2002 – which, as mentioned above, means a $1,000,000 exemption and 55% estate tax rate.*[13]

Get a will and a trust. Get a durable power of attorney, which allows your spouse or another person to make financial decisions on your behalf in the event you become mentally or physically unable to do so. Also, get a "health care proxy," which allows you to make decisions in advance about your health care and determines who can make decisions for you in the event you become incapacitated.

You should also make sure your parents are taking care of business because if they die without doing so, their business becomes your business! You need to have a very open discussion about life and death issues. Ask your parents if they have insurance and a will. Ask them their feelings about going into a nursing home or what they would like to be done should they be incapacitated. Find out if they have preferences regarding cremation or burial. Many of these things seem morbid to address while you are still alive and well, but if you choose not to talk about them, you may have to make decisions for your parents without knowing their choices. The same is true for your spouse and children—if you don't discuss these things with them, they may have to make decisions on your behalf without your input.

HEALTH INSURANCE

A recent study by Kaiser Family Foundation showed that nearly one in five Americans under age 64 has no healthcare insurance coverage whatsoever. How can you get health insurance? You can either get coverage through an employer healthcare plan or you find your own plan. There are two major types of healthcare plans—fee-for-service (indemnity plan) and managed care plan.

Fee-for-service plans are more expensive with higher deductibles because you are able to choose your healthcare specialist without anyone's approval; in other words, you are not forced to choose from a list of doctors. Managed care plans are more popular because they are less expensive and easier to use. You must choose your primary care physician from a list of doctors. There are three types of managed care plans: HMOs (health maintenance organizations), PPOs (preferred provider organizations; these cost more than HMOs), and POSs (point-of-service; this is the most expensive option, costing more than PPOs). Buy the best healthcare insurance you can afford; don't take any chances with your health, for your own sake and your family's.

LIFE INSURANCE

There are two main ways you can get life insurance—get coverage through an employer or find your own plan (buy the best life insurance you can afford). There are two major types, term and permanent life insurance.

Term life insurance is a simple and cheap protection plan and can be *annual renewable term* where the death benefit remains the same but the premiums get larger each year. It provides coverage at a fixed rate of payments for a limited period of time, the relevant term. After that period expires, coverage at the previous rate of premiums is no longer guaranteed and the client must either forgo coverage or obtain further coverage with different payments and/or conditions.

Some types of life insurance which are considered to be *permanent life insurance* policies are whole life insurance, universal life, and variable life. *Whole life insurance* is permanent life insurance with a guaranteed death benefit which remains level for as long as the policy is in force. It can never be canceled by the life insurance company. *Universal life insurance* is a combination of term life insurance coupled with a saving element. A universal life insurance can be described as an adjustable benefit life insurance with flexible premiums. It is complicated and should only be considered if your income is more than $100,000 a year and you have fully utilized all other tax deferred retirement plans. *Variable life insurance* allows you to invest the bulk of your premiums in one or more investment funds such as stocks, bonds, money markets, etc. You also have the right to switch from one investment to another, and it has a guaranteed death benefit.

When buying insurance, remember that whole life insurance (or permanent insurance) costs more than term life. With term life insurance, you are buying "just in case" insurance. Term life insurance provides coverage for a limited period of time. After that period the insured can either drop the policy or pay annually increasing premiums to continue the coverage. Term life costs less than whole life insurance and has no cash value. Whole life costs more and has cash value; it pays the face amount of the policy. Term insurance is recommended by most financial advisors if you are not purchasing it for investment.

Life insurance is available for purchase on the Internet by a number of reputable companies: Ameritax (www.ameritax.com), Master Quote of America, Inc. (www.masterquote.com), E-INSURE Services, Inc. (www.einsurance.com), Quotesmith.com Inc. (www.quotesmith.com), and InsWeb Corp. (www.insweb.com). Make sure you get the life insurance coverage you need. Calculate the amount of insurance needed.

If you need a monthly income of $1,800, you will need an insurance policy to cover the income in the event your spouse dies. To determine how much coverage you need, take your monthly income needed ($1,800) and first divide it by 500 (= 3.6). Multiply that answer by $100,000 to determine the needed death benefit of your insurance policy. In other words, you will need a death benefit policy in the amount of $360,000 in the event your spouse dies.

What DO you do should your spouse die? Be prepared. What will you do when you receive a $360,000 lump sum death benefit payment? Should you spend the death benefit payment without having a plan? No. The right answer is to be prepared to act responsibly with the $360,000 death benefit paid to you.

Plan now before a death occurs. Have a plan to invest a portion of the death benefit payment into an income fund and a portion in a growth fund. For example, if you are paid $360,000 in a death benefit payment, you need to do two different calculations to continue to pay your monthly expenses ($1,800) and make a contribution in a future growth fund. You should calculate the amount of the $360,000 you should invest to receive $900 income to help pay your expenses of $1,800 per month. You do this by multiplying $900 (the amount of income you lost when your spouse died) by 12 months (= $10,800), the amount of income you will need per year for monthly income. Divide 100 by 6 = 17. Multiply $10,800 by 17 = $183,600, the amount you will need to invest for income purposes. Now, subtract $360,000 - $183,600 = $176,400, the amount you will need to invest in a growth fund for the future.

Remember, be prepared! The death benefit payment is a gift from God; what you do with the $360,000 death benefit payment is your gift to God.

DISABILITY AND LONG-TERM CARE INSURANCE

One out of every ten people will have to cope with a severe disability. If you are still working and you suffer an incapacitating disability, you need disability insurance to replace your current take-home income. Do your homework first! Ask your employer about disability insurance coverage. It should pay you 60% of your current gross income until you turn 65 should you become disabled.

If you are in your 60s, it's time to consider long-term care insurance. Long-term care benefits will be paid only if your doctor says you have a medical necessity, are not able to perform activities of daily living, or have a cognitive impairment such as Alzheimer's disease. There are many long-term care providers available such as GE Financial Assurance (www.gefn.com), John Hancock Life Insurance (www.jhancock.com), or Long Term Care (LTC) Insurance (www.ltcinsurance.com). There is a huge difference in price among insurance companies, and the cost of long-term care increases with age. You will have to shop around. Long Term Care does not have a fixed rate, and many factors might contribute to the cost. The amount of money you might pay can change depending on what state you're in, the facility you choose and the degree of attention. Nursing homes, though they generally charge a month at a time, calculate their cost by how much money is required per day. A long-term care insurance policy might refer to "daily benefits," since it also determines the amount of money you will receive in terms of daily cost. A nursing home can charge anywhere from $100 to $300 a day. The nature and quality of the facility will also vary. Home care will also be calculated daily, but generally do not cost as much as a nursing home or other facility. [14]

When choosing a long-term care insurance company, ask a long-term care insurance professional, not a salesperson. Find someone who has been in the business for at least 10 years and then ask the following questions:

- What does the policy cover?

- How much will the policy pay out in daily benefits?

- When will my benefits kick in, and how long will they last?

- Will I have to still pay premiums while in the nursing care facility?

- Are there diseases or injuries that are not covered?

- What is your rating from the independent companies that rate the safety and soundness of all insurance carriers?

If the agent states he/she doesn't know the ratings, take your business elsewhere. The following companies rate insurance providers: AM Best (908-439-2200), Moody's (212-553-0377), Standard & Poor's (212-208-8000), DUFF and Phelps (312-263-2610), and Weiss (www.WeissRatings.com).

Wealth Check-Up

Which of the following best describes your financial responsibility?

❑ I have a will.

❑ I need someone to help me get my will updated.

❑ I was told I don't need a will because I don't have very many assets.

❑ I have a revocable living trust.

❑ I need someone to help me get my trust updated.

❑ I was told I don't need a trust because I don't have very many assets.

❑ I have long-term care insurance to cover my expenses should I be placed in a nursing home.

❑ I have health insurance.

❑ I was told I don't need long-term care insurance because I don't plan to go to a nursing home.

❏ I have life insurance.

❏ I was told I don't need life insurance because I am over 65.

❏ I am under 65 and I need life insurance.

❏ I have long-term disability insurance.

STEP SEVEN: REST

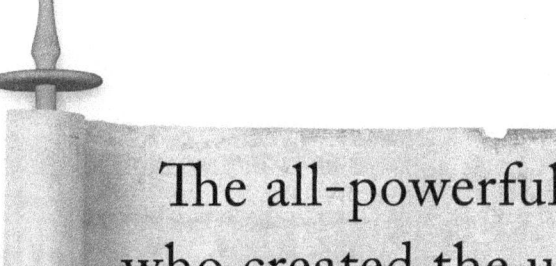

The all-powerful God who created the universe and keeps it running can take care of YOUR financial problems. **Believe!**

Accept the Gift

STEP SEVEN WILL BE THE FINAL STEP OF our spiritual journey. Our work is complete! Step Seven will be a time of accepting God's gifts. In this Step, we accept God's plan for putting your financial goals in spiritual alignment. In this step, God puts us in the perfect place to find peace, abundance and freedom to extend acts of kindness to others in need. This step is a time to enjoy who God is and do what He has asked you to do, using Biblical principles, to correct "bad" spending habits. I am honored to have had this opportunity to be your personal motivator. I hope you have enjoyed our journey through the previous six steps.

Step Seven has extreme significance to our spiritual journey to financial freedom. There are times when our financial situation may seem hopeless. At times like this we need *physical and spiritual* rest to go forward. Rest is more than just sleep alone. Rest empowers! It empowers us to serve others by offering acts of kindness to those in need. Rest means a total surrender to God's care and protection.

When we began our *spiritual* journey to check our emotions in Step One, we never intended for you to go it alone. Jesus himself found out firsthand when He became a human being that He needed to depend heavily on His heavenly Father for support and guidance. When He was exhausted, He went off by Himself to rest in God. You have worked very hard in Steps One through Six. *"Six days do your work, but on the seventh day do not work, so that your ox and your donkey may rest and the slave born in your household, and the alien as well, may be refreshed"* (Exodus 23:12 NIV).

Be refreshed! We will not do any work so that you may be refreshed in Step Seven. In steps one to six, you did the work. You may feel exhausted after learning how to get your emotions and finances in order: resolving unpaid bills, negotiating a reduced pay-off debt balance, and requesting negative comments to be removed from your credit report. You now know the action steps to take if you are in financial trouble: be proactive, investigate, and pay off your credit cards (the worst kind of debt you can have) by prioritizing your cards with the highest interest rates first to give you an incentive to continue to pay down your expenses.

Step Seven is the prescription for our physical, material, and spiritual health: Rest, our final step. Now is the time to celebrate! Celebrate your success for the work you accomplished in Step One through Step Six of this book. In this final step of our seven-step spiritual journey, we will focus on the Biblical principles to help you achieve physical and spiritual rest.

When you accept the gift of God's rest, you take a break from your financial troubles. You don't tell God what to do or how to do it. *"For nothing is impossible with God"* (Luke 1:37 NIV). Rest means turning our finances over to God to let him fix it. He promised to do just that: *"Come to me all you who are weary and burdened, and I will give you rest"* (Matthew 11:28 NIV).

- Rest means not giving up.

- Rest means not giving in to despair.

- Rest means trusting.

- Rest means surrendering, not interfering.

- Rest means having so much faith in God that we can finally have some peace.

- Rest means believing that the all-powerful God who created the universe and keeps it running can take care of our financial problems.

- Rest means obedience, returning a faithful tithe, and offering to the Lord.

- Rest means giving acts of financial kindness to others in need.

To our surprise, at the end of our final step, we're calm. Our anxiety is gone. To rest in God means exactly that: *rest!* Stress-free! Finally, we are now safe in the Master's hands, not MasterCard's. We've learned how to surrender to His care and protection, to let go and rest. I hope you have enjoyed this journey through *Finances & Spirituality*. May this final step of our seven-step journey be a bright and rewarding experience for many years to come.

A Biblical Principle:
Inspiration to Help You Meet Your Financial Goals

BE WISE WITH GOD'S GIFT

"There was a rich man whose manager was accused of wasting his possessions. So he called him in and asked him, 'What is this I hear about you? Give an account of your management, because you cannot be manager any longer'" (Luke 16: 1-2 NIV).

> *In an article "What the Gambling Industry Won't Tell You" (Reader's Digest, March 2001, p. 156 ff), Brian O'Keefe, lists six reasons why, as he puts it, "You're not just losing, you're being taken." They are, implies the casino industry:*
>
> - *You can't win*
> - *When you think you've won, we might not pay you*

> - *Addicts keep us in the money*
> - *Your children are getting hooked*
> - *And so are your parents*
> - *We've got legislators in our pocket*
>
> *How we handle God's resources placed in our trust may not only affect us each individually, but may also affect those around us – children, parents, friends, etc. Being a good steward of God's resources means: expressing honesty, by returning the tithes that belong to God, and also by giving as we are able."* [15]

God, who has given us life, knows that we need food to sustain it. He created our bodies, so He knows we need clothing. He knows we need food. Jesus tells us in Matthew 6:25 (NIV), *"Therefore I tell you, do not worry about your life, what you will eat or drink; or about your body, what you will wear. Is not life more than food, and the body more than clothes?"*

Accept the precious gift which God gives you for the ability to produce wealth – not for building an earthly treasure of greed, but your ability to produce wealth to be a good steward to your family, church, and community. Throughout our time together, we focused on using Biblical principles to correct "bad" money habits, attitudes and behaviors to "do good" things for ourselves and others. However, there can be no "rest" when the love of money is treasured in our hearts. There can be no "rest," only worry, confusion, and stress as the treasures pursued quickly disappear when we allow our possessions and power to rule our hearts. We can only have "rest" when we accept God's free gift. Remember Jesus's message in Matthew 11:28 NIV: *"Come to me all you who are weary and burdened, and I will give you rest."*

Accept God's rest. Rest in the understanding that you understand what it means to have the support and guidance from the Father. Rest means the creditors will not be coming to take you and your family as slaves because God's provision is as large as your faith and your willingness to obey. *"Indeed, the very hairs of your head are all numbered. Don't be afraid; you are worth more than many sparrows"* (Luke 12:7 NIV).

The message is this: Take responsible action to get your finances in order! Don't worry; trust God. Believe you will achieve peace, abundance and financial freedom through God's provision as large as your faith.

NOW IS THE TIME TO TAKE ACTION

Do something special for God! Take Action -

- Be accountable: Know where you stand.

- Be responsible for your family's future: Get a will and trust and procure enough insurance for your family's needs.

- Be responsible: Don't blame anyone else for your financial situation.

- Build an emergency fund by having a cash cushion worth six months of expenses.

- Create a budget and live below your means.

- Invest a portion of your after-tax income (10% to 15%).

- Make a decision to pay off your debt.

- Make savings a priority.

- Negotiate a reduced balance to pay-off loans and credit card debt.

- Put some money away before you see it.

- Request negative comments to be removed from your credit report.

- Spend less each paycheck.

- Spend only what you can afford!

You have the ability to produce abundant wealth! Ask for help, *"And my God will meet all your needs according to his glorious riches"* (Philippians 4:19 NIV).

Your Money Matters
DISCOVER HOW YOUR MONEY COULD BE DOING MORE

DON'T PANIC

There is no need to panic about your finances! Spend less each paycheck! Put some of your money away before you see it! Spend only what you can afford! …

Rest means to…

- Surrender EVERYTHING to God's care and protection.

- Serve others by offering acts of kindness to those in need.

The spiritual gift of rest is God's gift of wealth to us; what you do with that wealth is your gift *to* God. You have the ability to produce abundant wealth! Ask for help, *"And my God will meet all your needs according to his glorious riches"* (Philippians 4:19 NIV). Ask for rest, *"…and you will find rest"* (Matthew 11:29 NIV).

Until we meet again along the journey … Be wise with God's spiritual and material gifts.

NEXT STEP

SERVE THE WORLD

Is there anyone more competent than God when many families are facing financial distress due to high debt burdens? No. Is there anyone more competent than God when our household wealth is being squandered? *"Not long after that, the younger son got together all he had, set off for a distant country and there squandered his wealth in wild living"* (Luke 15:13 NIV). The message is this: Don't squander God's gifts in excessive living. Do something special for God by reaching out to a neighbor, praying for a hurting friend, or encouraging a student, parent or senior citizen.

Now is a good time to express your love to God and to others in need. Reach out! Reach across! Identify the needs of others in your community. We have this unexplainable assurance God is the shelter in the time of any financial storm, that everything about our finances is going to turn out all right, even if we have more work to do. We must believe that God will be with us and He will take care of us, any time we ask. You can serve others knowing that your request for financial help has been heard. Extend acts of kindness to others in financial need! Through acts of kindness we reflect the character of Christ to those around us. Recapture the word "service" and all that it implies!

A Final Note

Dear Friends,

Thank you for taking this journey with me – seven spiritual steps to finding peace, abundance, and financial freedom in your personal finances. It is God and God alone who gives us the power to have peace, abundance, and freedom in life. That's wealth! And when God gives wealth to us, we deserve to have it!

We began our journey with the joy of acknowledging God's ownership. We learned that God not only gives us money and material possessions but our body, time, and abilities. God entrusts us to be a good steward of all He has given us because He is the source of every good and perfect gift. The Bible says that God will order our "steps" until we achieve financial success. I pray that you have enjoyed reading this book.

If you had financial troubles before you took the first step in our wealth journey, it is my prayer that by the time you reach Step Seven, you will have claimed the power that comes from paying your debts and living within your means. If you still have financial troubles today, there is no need to panic! We all have some bad money habits, but it is quite possible that the cure you need most is the help you will receive from faith in Jesus Christ.

Remember to ... Check Your Emotions! – Step One ... Be Honest! – Step Two ... Get Control! – Step Three ... DO GOOD! – Step Four ... Pay for Your Future! – Step Five ... Be Responsible! – Step Six ... and Step Seven – Rest!

Remember to .... Believe in God's power to help you get control of your finances. He will give you the peace and abundance you need to take care of your family and serve others in need.

Finances & Spirituality is God's perfect seven-step plan to finding peace, abundance, and freedom in your personal finances.

Remember ... God is the only one who gives us the power and abilities to produce wealth, pay our debts, and have enough money left over to support ourselves, our families, and others in need with the rest that is left after we return a faithful tithe and offering. I encourage you to retrain your thinking and believe that God can do what He says He will do. He says in His Word that He will give you power to find peace, abundance, and freedom in your personal finances. Claim His power and be blessed!

With Deepest Affection,
   Doris

ENDNOTES

[1] *First Quarter Adult Bible Study Guide.* (2011). Nampa, ID: Pacific Press Publishing Association, p. 132.

[2] Kromminga, A.G. (2005). *2005 Stewardship Readings*, Silver Springs, MD: NAD Stewardship Publications.

[3] Visual Economics. (2010). *How the average U.S. consumer spends their paycheck.* Retrieved from http://visual.ly/how-average-consumer-spends-their-paycheck

[4] Kromminga, p.19.

[5] American Household Credit Card Debt Statistics through 2012 by Tim. *Credit card statistics, industry facts, debt statistics.* Retrieved from http://www.nerdwallet.com/blog/credit-card data/average-credit-card-debt-household/

⁶ Wang, J (2012, April 27) *Historical Average Tax Refund*. Retrieved from http://www.bargaineering.com/articles/average-tax-refund.html

⁷ Fetterman, M., & Hansen, B. (2006, November 26). Young people struggle to deal with kiss of debt. *USA Today*. Retrieved from http://www.usatoday.com/money/perfi/credit/2006-11-19-young-and-in-debt-cover_x.htm

⁸ Johnson, A., & Brown, F. (2007, March 14). Call for "Gen Y" to get credit-wise. *Veda Advantage*. Retrieved from http://www.b2bay.com.au/latest_news/geny_to_get_credit_wise.aspx

⁹ Kromminga, p.5.

¹⁰ Thomas, J.D. (2009). *Blessings: A contemporary adaptation of Ellen White's class work Thoughts from the Mount of Blessing*. Nampa, ID: Pacific Press, p. 43.

¹¹ Kromminga, p.40.

¹² Kromminga, p.35.

¹³ Garber, J. (2011). What is the future of the federal estate tax? *About.com*. Retrieved from http://wills.about.com/od/understandingestatetaxes/a/futureoftax.htm?p=1

[14] LTC Insurance Company. (2011). *What can you expect to pay for your long term care insurance policy?* Retrieved from http://www.ltcinsurance.com/long-term-care-insurance-costs.html

[15] Kromminga, p.9.

References

American Household Credit Card Debt Statistics through 2012 by Tim. *Credit card statistics, industry facts, debt statistics.* Retrieved from http://www.nerdwallet.com/blog/credit-card-data/average-credit-card-debt-household/

Fetterman, M., & Hansen, B. (2006, November 26). Young people struggle to deal with kiss of debt. *USA Today.* Retrieved from http://www.usatoday.com/money/perfi/credit/2006-11-19-young-and-in-debt-cover_x.htm

First Quarter Adult Bible Study Guide. (2011). Nampa, ID: Pacific Press Publishing Association.

Garber, J. (2011). What is the future of the federal estate tax? *About.com.* Retrieved from http://wills.about.com/od/understandingestatetaxes/a/futureoftax.htm?p=1

Johnson, A., & Brown, F. (2007, March 14). Call for "Gen Y" to get credit-wise. *Veda Advantage.* Retrieved from http://www.b2bay.com.au/latest_news/geny_to_get_credit_wise.aspx

Krominga, A.G. (2005). *2005 Stewardship Readings*, Silver Springs, MD: NAD Stewardship Publications.

LTC Insurance Company. (2011). *What can you expect to pay for your long term care insurance policy?* Retrieved from http://www.ltcinsurance.com/long-term-care-insurance-costs.html

Thomas, J.D. (2009). *Blessings: A contemporary adaptation of Ellen White's class work Thoughts from the Mount of Blessing.* Nampa, ID: Pacific Press.

Visual Economics. (2010). *How the average U.S. consumer spends their paycheck.* Retrieved from http://www.visualeconomics.com/how-the-average-us-consumer-spends-their-paycheck/

Wang, J (2012, April 27) *Historical Average Tax Refund.* Re-trieved from http://www.bargaineering.com/articles/average-tax-refund.html

Woolsey, B., & Schultz, M. (2011, February 11). Credit card statistics, industry facts, debt statistics. *Creditcards.com.* Retrieved from http://www.creditcards.com/credit-card-news/credit-card-industry-facts-personal-debt-statistics-1276.php

www.ingramcontent.com/pod-product-compliance
Lightning Source LLC
LaVergne TN
LVHW041620070426
835507LV00008B/348